Make It Happen

Make It Happen

The Prince's Trust Guide to Starting Your Own Business

Prince's Trust

CAPSTONE

This edition first published 2011
© 2011 The Prince's Trust

First edition published 2011 by Capstone Publishing Ltd (A Wiley Company)

Registered office
The Atrium, Southern Gate, Chichester, West Sussex, PO19 8SQ, United Kingdom

For details of our global editorial offices, for customer services and for information about how to apply for permission to reuse the copyright material in this book please see our website at www.wiley.com.

Library of Congress Cataloguing-in-Publication Data
is available

ISBN: 9780857080455
Ebook: 8780857081360

A catalogue record for this book is available from the British Library.

Set in 10/16 pt Swiss 721 BT Light by Sparks – www.sparkspublishing.com
Printed in [Country] by [Printer]

FSC
www.fsc.org
MIX
Paper from
responsible sources
FSC® C015829

Contents

CLARENCE HOUSE

It gives me great pleasure to introduce this book, which has been developed in partnership with my Trust. It aims to spread some of the practical insights and inspirational stories which demonstrate that the United Kingdom is alive with enterprise.

When I founded The Prince's Trust Enterprise Programme in 1983, my sincere wish was that disadvantaged young people should have more opportunities to realize their potential. I hoped that by providing advice, guidance and basic financial support, young people could transform their lives by creating successful businesses. Back then, I could scarcely have imagined the scale of what we might achieve. To date, my Trust has helped launch more than 70,000 new businesses and it continues to support 100 more young people each and every working day.

Many of the young people we meet have great potential, but lack the confidence and motivation to turn their ideas into reality. If, like many of them, you have an idea for a business, but don't know where to start, I can only encourage you to read this book. It aims to share some of the knowledge and inspirational stories which my Trust has collected throughout the years. Much is based on our experience of working with some exceptional young people who have overcome great adversity to achieve extraordinary success.

I am most grateful to all of our supporters who have contributed to this book, including Andrew Dixon, Ben White, Claire Locke, James Caan, Tim Roupell, Sarah Tremellen, Nick Jenkins, Geoff Quinn, Tony Elliott and Mike Clare. As well as providing their own fascinating business insights, they each commit endless time and energy to supporting the work of my Trust. I owe particular thanks to Charles Dunstone, an indefatigable and passionate Chairman who champions the cause of the most needy young people throughout the United Kingdom.

I am also indebted to all of the young people whose stories bring this book to life in such a vivid way. Whenever I hear of their achievements, I feel such a sense of pride. Their enterprising spirit has not only changed their lives and created a brighter future for their families, it has also made an important contribution to the economic well-being of our entire nation.

I am delighted to say that a sum of the proceeds from the sales of this book will go towards supporting the work of my Trust. This, in turn, will help us to support even more young people and encourage the next generation of young entrepreneurs.

Foreword

Charles Dunstone

All of us, without exception, have one idea that got away. There may be a number of reasons why an idea might flounder – little time, knowledge, motivation or confidence. As Chairman, I can say that what The Prince's Trust does best is to back the idea.

The Trust's Enterprise Programme allows young people to explore the potential of their business ideas and more importantly to discover their own potential for success. Time and time again, I am impressed by the entrepreneurial spirit of the young people whom The Prince's Trust helps. This book goes some way to demonstrating that young people today are resilient, creative and enterprising – and after reading their stories I hope you will feel inspired to follow in their footsteps.

Running your own business is tough, demanding, frustrating and incredibly hard work. It is also the most satisfying, life affirming and rewarding thing you can do. We help people not only build great enterprises; we help them rebuild their life and self-respect by creating and owning something they feel passionate about. I am very proud to play my small part in their success.

We are hugely grateful to RBS for their support of the Enterprise Programme and their generosity in making this book available to young people over the coming three years. Their support should mean that the advice and inspiration offered in this book makes a difference where it is needed most.

Foreword

Lisa Dunlop, Beauty Secrets

I had no interest in school and left without qualifications. I got a few small jobs, working in a chip shop and hairdressers and things like that. When I was 18, I got into an abusive relationship with a man and had my first child with him. He ended up in prison and is still there. I went back and did a beauty course. I also did a business course and was aiming to set up my own business. But I was by then in another relationship, and had a baby that died. I had post-natal depression and was grieving for the baby. I fell pregnant again, but found out that my partner was going to have a baby with someone else, who was pregnant at the same time. He took up with her and I felt totally rejected. When Lewis was born, I had really bad post-natal depression again. I was so angry. I didn't want to be on my own with two kids by two different people. Nobody wants that. I was angry with myself, and embarrassed and humiliated that my partner was with someone else. I was having a breakdown and needed to get professional help but I didn't. I didn't leave the house for two years. I would forget to eat and just cry every night.

One night, I wrote a letter to God saying 'take me home'. I had everything planned, even what clothes they should put on me when I died.

I woke up the next morning and thought, 'Why am I still here?' I walked downstairs and there was a letter saying that I had enquired about a business unit two to three years ago, that one was now available, and did I want to have a look at it? Something made me say, 'just go'.

I agreed to take it even though I had no money, and then applied to The Prince's Trust and got my loan. My family lent me the rest of the money and I set the whole thing up. My beauty salon was open in eight weeks.

The Prince's Trust is not just financial support. They actually believe in you. Your mind tries to sabotage things, and you start doubting yourself, but they don't. It's as if they can see it in you. They give you confidence and feedback when you are unsure of yourself or your ideas and help you achieve your dreams. Up until then, my life had been about rejection and thinking I wasn't good enough because of the way people treated me.

My life is completely different now to how it was 18 months ago. I was entered into a competition by The Prince's Trust, and I was so proud of myself because I had really achieved something. I have two beauticians and receptionists working for me. I have not just set up my salon, but am taking it to the next stage, where I will have spiritual gifts and essential oils at the front. If things take off, I will open up a second premises. Eventually I would like to have my own school where I will teach beauty and complementary therapy. I feel now I can do whatever I want. I will never go back to where I was, never.

'Turn your business dreams into reality'

Introduction

Make It Happen takes you through the different stages of setting up your own business, starting with researching your original idea through to expanding your successful business. Each of the chapters covers specific areas that you will need to consider, and is packed with advice, not just on what to do when, but how to do it. You can't beat first-hand experience and in each chapter you will find case studies from young people who have taken the self-employed route themselves, and who provide real insight into what setting up a business is really like. There are also suggestions from successful business people who have been there, done that, and are here to tell you how.

The last chapter looks at how to put together a business plan. This will help you check that everything is in place for setting up your business, having thought through the points raised in the rest of the book.

At the back of the book you will find a directory for further information. There is a wealth of information out there for people wanting to start a business, and you should take full advantage of it.

We hope that you enjoy reading *Make It Happen*, and that it acts as the driver for you to take that first step into turning your business dreams into reality.

'Building a business starts with you'

one

Starting a business

Starting your own business will be one of the most exciting and challenging things you will ever do. To be successful, you'll need to be well prepared for what lies ahead. Careful planning will help you turn a great idea into a profitable reality.

Is running a business for you?

Whatever your starting point, there are some basic questions you need to ask yourself about your business idea, your personal aims, your skills and your know-how.

Running a business is challenging and time-consuming, so it's worth thinking about whether this labour of love would suit your personality and lifestyle. Having your own business and seeing the direct impact (and hopefully benefit!) of every decision you make can be incredibly rewarding. But being your own boss means that the buck stops with you, which can make it harder to switch off at 5pm or weekends. It's a good idea to speak to people who have been there and done it; ask them their reasons for being self-employed, what they hoped to gain, whether it has been all they expected and what their plans are for the future. There is no better way to judge whether self-employment is right for you than to seek advice directly from those already doing it. Be brave too. Ask local business owners about the highs and lows of running their own business. The better prepared you are to visualise yourself coping with challenges – as well as with successes – the more easily you will be able to answer the question: is running a business right for me?

'Building a business starts with you'

Entrepreneur's checklist

There is no one type of person who is good at running a business but there are some characteristics that successful small business owners have in common. Andrew Dixon, the founder of ARC InterCapital, and Claire Locke, the founder of clothes brand Artigiano, suggest these are some of the most important traits:

➔ **Passion and drive** – will it keep you up at night thinking how to improve your business? Do you care enough?

➔ **Focus and determination** – you don't need to be particularly clever to start a business. You do need these traits – in spades.

➔ **Creative streak** – not in terms of artistic flair, but more imagination as to how you can differentiate yourself from competitors, and take a fresh look at an established market.

➔ **Hard work** – you have to be prepared to put in the hours and be able to juggle a lot of balls at the same time.

➔ **Leadership skills** – can you motivate others to share your passion and follow your lead? There are a lot of good managers, but it is a real skill to be able to excite people. And that goes for customers as well as staff.

➔ **Put the customer first** – it is easy to get wrapped up in your business and do what you think the customer wants rather than what the customer actually wants. You need to be able to focus on the customer, who they are, and what problem you are solving for them. To do this, it helps to have good social skills and be able to empathise.

➔ **Paranoia** – in so much as you should always be aware of competitors.

➜ **Positive frame of mind** – whatever has happened the day before, you need to be able to wake up and put on a fresh pair of glasses, and have the ability and enthusiasm to overcome difficulties.

➜ **Resilience** – every day is to do with solving problems – can you keep going, and not be tempted to give up?

➜ **Risk and reward** – can you cope with both?

Don't worry if you haven't got all of these characteristics – it doesn't mean your business won't be a success. The key is to recognise the skills you have, the skills you need and how you are going to start filling in the gaps.

What do you want to achieve?

Not all people will start a business because they want the power and wealth of Bill Gates. While some will be driven by money, others want to be their own boss to enjoy more creative freedom or the opportunity to improve the community around them. The reason that you go into business will affect the type of company that you become, so it is important to think of this at the start.

What's the big idea?

Building a business starts with you and your personality, your skills and your ideas. These three things are not set in stone; you will develop and change, as will your skills and ideas, and you will have plenty of opportunity to review each as time goes on. But it is important that you are clear about where you stand on all three before you start planning.

Are you clear about what your business will do? This may seem obvious but many people, brimming with ideas, overlook the importance of this question. Your business will need to stand out from the crowd if it is going to be noticed by customers. And that can be hard when, more likely than not, your customers will already be able to buy whatever you are offering elsewhere. There are very few genuinely new offerings. But don't panic, because you can still be a successful business without a unique product or service.

You need to create a Unique Selling Point (**USP**), a reason why customers should buy from you rather than anyone else out there. To develop your USP, look at what you do and how you do it. It's often how a business does what it does that sets it apart.

Do you offer free delivery, or is there something special about your customer service, for example? Consider your customers – is there something special about them? For example, are they based all over the world; do they have values in common? What benefits do customers get from your business: price; good quality service; or perhaps your personality? Above all, make sure that you put yourself in your customers' shoes and check that your idea is something that they will actually want, rather than a dream or product that you have fallen in love with.

> **Top tip**
>
> → Think about everything you would like your business to be, e.g. innovative, customer-focused, creative.
>
> → Think about all of the skills, strengths and knowledge you will bring to your business.
>
> → Do both sides match?
>
> → Do you need to develop different skills?

Try to be as specific as possible about the kind of business you want to run. If you want to run a café/restaurant, will it just be open in the daytime or are you prepared to work evenings? Will it be traditional or innovative? It's one thing to know that you want to start a clothing label for example, but you need to be certain about what type of clothing label, attracting which sector of the market? What will be your input? What sort of customers are you expecting to have?

Decisions that you make about what your business is and isn't will affect every aspect of your venture – from your choice of premises and location, to the amount you will need to spend on fixtures and fittings.

'Your decisions about what your business is and isn't will affect every aspect of your venture'

Your business values

Now that you have your business idea and you have thought about what it is you are hoping to achieve, it's good to take a step back and think about the type of business you hope to run. The reason you are setting up your business and the type of business you hope to become will form a core part of your business – your business values. These values will probably be instinctive to you, and you will probably already have thought about them in trying to work out your USP.

For example, if your aim is to exceed a customer's expectations every time, and to provide outstanding customer service, that is an important business value, but it will also distinguish you from the competition and help you find your niche in the market.

What other values might you have – treating staff and customers with respect? Working to a consistently high standard on every job? While these things may be instinctive to you, it is worthwhile writing them down. Not only will this make it clearer to both you and your business partner or first employees, it will help a customer understand what they can expect of you. That will be the making of your brand (for more on brands and brand identity, see Chapter Two).

The second part of the exercise is to think about why you are in business. Is it important to you who might benefit from your company's success, or whether what you do will make a difference? If you do something of which you can be proud, and that benefits the community in which you work, there will also be benefits for you and your business. For starters, it will be easier to build up a strong reputation. It will also help you keep your focus and not get easily sidetracked. If you are clear on why you are in business, it will help you to pass on your vision to customers and staff. Again, writing those thoughts down will be helpful, so that you can communicate them more clearly to customers, future employees or potential investors. If you are clear about how you see your business you will find it easy to describe your business to other people. You will have plenty of opportunity to tell people about your business – you could be meeting potential customers at a bus stop, at your local pub, even in the back of a taxi. You need to make every opportunity that you have to talk about your business count.

You should also think about what your business is, in terms of what it stands for and, importantly, what your business isn't. This works in terms of both values for your business and the description of your business.

What my business is

My business will be known for stocking ethically produced clothing.

My business will provide quality materials at an affordable price.

What my business isn't

My business will never trade with suppliers who do not pay workers a fair wage.

My business is not high-street mass market.

Beyond business

If your business values show that the main aim of your business is to improve the community or environment around you, rather than make profit for yourself, it may be that your business will be a social enterprise. This is a business with primarily social objectives, where the majority of profits are reinvested for that purpose back into the business or community. Social enterprises are still run as successful businesses, but adopt socially and environmentally responsible approaches to buying and delivering services and products, or address a particular social or environmental need, e.g. by providing transport for schoolchildren, or recycling services. Examples include the Big Issue magazine, or The Eden Project. These enterprises can take different forms, which to a greater or lesser extent, can help with financing. These include: **Community Interest Companies**, where the social aims are checked and regulations are in place to stop the assets and profits being distributed for other purposes; charities, where tax breaks can be an advantage; and companies limited by shares.

My story

Jessie Jowers and Carlo Montesanti, Bee Guardian Foundation

We set up the Bee Guardian Foundation which runs the Global Bee Project in 2009, with the aim of educating people about the importance of all bee species.

We set up as a Community Interest Company (CIC) limited by guarantee. It meant that we as directors could run and make decisions for the project. We would be a limited company, registered at Companies House, but accountable to a regulating body – The CIC Regulator. Having CIC status means that we are not viewed as a money-making operation. You obviously have to turn a profit, but we are more concerned about getting a message and information across.

We didn't want to be funding dependent, but there is financial support for CICs as they come under the banner of social enterprises. It means that you can apply for particular grants.

It was important to us that people saw us as a CIC. People are sceptical of organisations that use an idea for profit. If you are looking for membership, as we are, people don't like to think that the money is going into a director's pockets. It helps if they know you are being regulated and the proceeds will be accounted for within the business.

By becoming a CIC, we tapped into a whole network of social entrepreneurs around the country. We could see how they set up their companies and we could learn from them. The CIC Regulator promotes networking opportunities, and has been a great help. The staff were very knowledgeable, gave good advice and also have a fantastic website.

Being a CIC can provide a middle ground between a charity and a traditional limited company. It is also good for tax purposes and can create better funding opportunities.

Researching the big idea

Unless, and until, you start researching your market, talking to potential customers and studying competitors, you cannot be sure that people really will want what you're trying to sell. Thorough **market research** is crucial. And the more research you do, the easier it will be in the future to make decisions about your marketing strategy, pricing, budget and sales targets. It will also help you to identify where there are gaps in your knowledge or skills.

Market research will help you to identify:

➔ whether there is a market for your product or service

➔ how much demand there will be for your product or service

➔ who your target customers are in terms of age, gender, location, profession, income, where they currently buy your product or service

➔ how you will reach your target customers

➔ how much your product or service is worth to your target customers and how often they will buy

➔ who your competitors will be.

A good starting point is to find out as much as you can about your target customers and competitors by reading local newspapers, market reports, trade magazines and business directories, surfing the internet and interviewing your potential customers and business owners in your market.

What worked for me

Ben White, Notion Capital

When I was 16, I persuaded my father to lend me some money in order to buy a load of Christmas trees and sell them door-to-door. Unfortunately, it was the week before Christmas and most people had already bought theirs! However, of those that I did sell, it was an amazing feeling, one that I still find fantastic to this day. You either enjoy talking to people and selling them stuff, or you don't, I believe it is a trait that you are born with. You can get better at it, but you can't learn to love it.

Whatever your business is, you need a selling element. It won't stop you being an entrepreneur if you can't do it well, but you will need to team up with someone who can. A person's biggest strength is knowing their own weakness and being upfront about it.

When you're thinking up your big idea, ask yourself 'Does it solve real problems? What does it do? Why will people pay for it?!' Take a concept to people and ask, 'If I can do something that would solve these problems, would you buy it?' The trick is to listen to people's problems and come up with a solution or look to sell a product or service that other companies are either doing badly or could be done differently.

With our company MessageLabs, we saw that anti-virus software sat on a desktop and was manually updated every month. But viruses come into a business from the internet, down one pipe. For example, if you turn your tap on, you expect the water to be clean.

In the same way if you turn your internet on, the same thing should apply, without you having to do the equivalent of boiling the water. So we looked at solving that problem in a more efficient and cost effective way by moving the antivirus software from the end user's desktop to the 'cloud'.

Market research is very important, but you can also save a lot of time and money by doing test runs. Try your product or idea on people and see what they think. It costs little, and you will learn an awful lot. Once you have done your market research and you have good reason to be confident, then have complete belief from that point. Being a little naïve can be a good thing. People become cynical and they will tell you to 'get a proper job'. But be confident, put your foot down, your blinkers on and make sure everyone stands aside! That belief in yourself and your product is infectious. You can do amazing things with a group of people if they all believe, and feel more than just a cog in a wheel. It's worth telling everyone in the business the whole story, so that they understand what you are doing, where you are going and everyone can feel a part of the journey.

Top tip

Be careful not to conduct market research on family and friends who are likely to tell you what you want to hear!

You could also try **test marketing** your idea, which is a great way to check out what people think of it and whether it will work. Test marketing your product or service doesn't have to be complicated or expensive. You could pick a spot near your potential business location to show your product to potential customers – giving away a free sample with a flyer about your business is a good way to get their attention. Or you could ask a local shop to carry a limited range of your product to see how customers respond, or even take out a market stall yourself. This will give you valuable feedback from real-life customers. You could also draw up a questionnaire that you can use to get customers' views either over the phone or by stopping them in the street. Testing out your product or idea on the public will show whether or not they will buy it, how much they would be willing to pay, which features are good or bad, and even whether they would bother travelling to get it. You could then make any adjustments you need to before you actually launch your business.

SWOT up

Test marketing your idea will help with potential customers but you also need to get to know your competitors. The best way is to talk to people, but try looking online or at the library as well. Once you've gathered your competitor information together, you should organise it – a useful way to do that is with a **SWOT** analysis. Don't be alarmed by the name – it's actually really simple to use. It stands for:

→ **Strengths** – where your business or your competitors are strong

→ **Weaknesses** – where your business or your competitors are weaker

→ **Opportunities** – developments available to your business or competitors

→ **Threats** – developments that could have a negative impact on your business or competitors.

A SWOT can be used to analyse your own business and that of your competitors. It is useful because it can help you to be impartial about your business and to look at it honestly. It will help you to consider internal and external things that might affect your business and to organise this information into categories. If you use a SWOT effectively, your competitors can help you to stay one step ahead of the game.

Strengths	Weaknesses
Opportunities	Threats

It's useful to do a SWOT when you're starting up, but don't stop there. Revisit your SWOT at least once a year as part of your planning for the next financial year of your business. With each coming year, strengths and weaknesses within your business will change, as they will for your competitors. Your business sector will also see new opportunities and threats develop, and it'll be up to you to keep up to speed and prepare your business for these changes.

Pricing

Getting the right price for your product or service is a crucial step. Price it too low and you may not make enough money to cover your costs, give yourself a salary and make a profit. Price it too high, and you may put customers off. Your market research will be handy here, as it is good to know what your competitors are charging. Armed with this information, think about how much you will need to sell to break even, i.e. cover your costs, and then add on the sum that will be your profit – the profit margin.

When deciding on the profit margin, think about what your product or service is worth to the customer. If your customer's pipes burst and there is water leaking, your service in fixing it and stopping more damage to the house will be worth more to the customer than just your travel expenses in getting there and an hour of your time.

Pricing can also be used as a marketing tool. The price you charge for a product or service will position you in the marketplace and against your competitors. Do you want your product to be seen as 'cheap and cheerful' or high-end, worth paying that bit more for?

Finding support

One of the most common complaints about self-employment is that it can be a lonely venture. You can often identify role models to motivate you, but it's less easy to find mentors to support you. An office worker, for example, can and does turn to colleagues for advice and guidance, a lot of the time without thinking. As someone starting a new business venture on their own, however, it can be difficult to know where to go for honest and constructive advice – particularly if none of your friends are in the same boat.

There are many reasons why you might want to consider finding a mentor. Not least, research proves that businesses that seek advice and support, particularly during start-up and their first few months of trading, are most likely to survive and succeed. You will often miss things when a business is your baby, and you can become tied up in the detail and miss the bigger picture. It's easy to start making decisions feeling you know best, when an outside perspective could prompt you to think about things you hadn't considered. It's also easy to feel de-motivated when you face a challenge you don't know how to deal with. Most importantly, it's useful to have someone you can call on to lend an impartial ear, give friendly advice and constructive criticism.

Some of the UK's most successful and best known entrepreneurs have mentors who have inspired, coached and guided them to where they are today.

'Some of the most successful entrepreneurs have had mentors who inspired and guided them'

My story

Mark Livsey, Founder, Parcel Partners

I had worked for a national distributor, and knew that transport and distribution would always be a growth industry. I wanted to set up my own logistics company. I knew what I needed to do to set it up, but was struggling with funding. I had my business plan and my first contract with Nightfreight, but it was still a real struggle to get funding. The banks wouldn't help and high interest loan companies were knocking me back, but I knew it would work. Then someone recommended The Prince's Trust to me, and they were brilliant and really quick.

I started in October 2007 with one van delivering to the same three postcodes every day. I can't drive, as I am disabled, so I had to get a driver and train him up. That meant that we weren't making money at the beginning. One contract wasn't enough to pay both of us. Now, I have over 20 staff, five sites and a fleet of 20 vehicles.

There was a low point when another carrier approached me to take on five rounds. We sorted everything on the phone, and I went to his offices to literally cross t's and dot i's. As soon as he saw I was disabled, the tone changed completely. He said he didn't realise I was so young and that the company had not been trading for long, but I knew what was really happening so walked out.

It could have suckerpunched anyone, but it just made me determined to do it all the more. Even my father said how can you go into an industry that is so physical? But I don't think a physical ailment can stop you doing anything. Believe in yourself and you can achieve anything. Doubt yourself and that's when things change.

If I wasn't doing this, I would really struggle. Work makes me happy. It's a hobby that I get paid for, not a job – so I guess I'd have to find another hobby.

Talk the talk

Community Interest Company (CIC)

This is a form of social enterprise that is regulated by a third party, the CIC Regulator, to ensure that its social aims are being met and profits reinvested for social purposes.

Market research

The steps you can take to work out whether there are customers out there that will buy your product or service.

Test marketing

A way of practising running your business.

USP

A Unique Selling Point is that X factor that means customers buy from your business above your competitors.

SWOT

A tool that will help you to assess your Strengths, Weaknesses, Opportunities and Threats as well as those of your competitors.

'Your business identity will affect who does and doesn't buy from you'

two

Forming a business

Now that you're clear on what your business will do and who your target market is, the next step is to actually set the business up and give it an identity. You'll need to decide on a name, a legal structure, and work out who you need to tell. But first of all, you'll need to make sure that you have enough money to get you going.

What will I need?

You will need enough money not only to cover the one-off costs of setting up your business, but also to cover your initial running costs, things like petrol, or electricity bills. If you don't have enough money yourself, you'll have to approach other sources of finance. This is where your market research is important, because potential funders will want to see that you have a realistic business proposal and have calculated the money needed to start up.

You also need to prove that you've thought about and planned your ongoing **budget**. Planning and sticking to a budget stops you from overspending, which is one of the main reasons why small businesses fail.

When you start to plan your business, think about:

→ **Start-up costs** – before you're in a position to start trading, you might have to buy stock, materials and equipment, lease premises or set up a website. Some of these things might require big spending before your business is even making any money. Where will this money come from?

→ **Personal living expenses** – the amount of money you will need to survive. It may be some months before you are able to take money out for yourself (**personal drawings**) from your business. Work out how much money you will need each month to cover the basics, such as rent or mortgage and bills, and whether you have this money or will need to take it from the business. As your business becomes established and your profits grow, you'll be able to take more money out of the business. To begin with, you'll probably want to re-invest most of your profits into building the business.

→ **Sales targets** – try to predict the sales you expect to make. Be realistic – a common problem for small businesses is that they run out of cash when they can't achieve ambitious sales targets.

Show me the money!

There are a number of options for financing your business. The two most common for small businesses are debt finance (such as a bank loan or overdraft) and grant funding.

→ **Start-up loan** – an amount of money you borrow from a bank and pay back over an agreed period and at an agreed rate of interest. Usually, loans are fairly flexible – you can pick a repayment period that suits your business and shop around for good deals. On the downside, loans often need to be guaranteed against an asset like a car or a property. Banks will usually want to see your business plan and a cash flow forecast, which will show how much money you expect to come in and go out of the business. You will also have to demonstrate to a bank manager that you have a back-up plan if your business does not earn as much as you planned in your cash flow forecast (for how to prepare a cash flow forecast, see Four).

→ **Overdraft** – when your bank agrees to let you take out more than you actually have in your account. Your bank will set a maximum level of overdraft. You only have to pay interest on the amount you are overdrawn, so overdrafts can be useful if you only need small amounts of extra cash regularly. However, the interest you pay is often higher than the rate for a loan, and the bank could demand repayment of the money you owe at any time.

→ **Grants** – a sum of money that usually doesn't have to be paid back. There are many grant schemes available to support small businesses. Grants are usually available in certain geographical areas, for certain types of businesses or for specific projects, like marketing or buying IT equipment. Although receiving money that does not need to be repaid is obviously attractive, grants are difficult to get hold of and competition for each one is intense. Applying for a scheme can be time-consuming and require a lot of paperwork. You're also sometimes asked to match the grant amount with your own money, which can be difficult for new businesses.

→ **Family and friends** – family or friends may be able to fully or part finance your venture. Even with family, it's a good idea to discuss these things properly. Will they want involvement in the business? Will they want a share of the profits? Remember, even the closest relationships can become strained where money is concerned. Agreeing terms in writing early on will help you to be open and honest about where everyone stands and what they can expect.

'Ask yourself whether you are prepared to compromise on your lifestyle'

Opening a business bank account

Before you can get hold of any money, you'll need to open a business bank account. It's best to do this once you have a business plan, as you will have an idea of the sales you might expect and what money you're likely to be dealing in, e.g. cash or cheques. If you already have a current account, talk to your bank about the business banking facilities they offer their customers. Some banks will offer a period of free banking to their existing customers. Don't be afraid to shop around. Banks offer very competitive business banking services, so it's worth seeing what's out there.

Opening a business bank account is fairly straightforward. You'll need:

→ a form of identification, such as your passport or driving licence

→ proof of your address, such as a recent gas or electricity bill.

It's also worth registering to vote by contacting your local council, as banks usually check for your name on the electoral role. It may cause problems if your name doesn't appear.

Bear in mind that a bank is likely to run a check on your credit history (**credit check**) before agreeing to give you an account. If you are currently paying off debts or have had debts in the past, this may affect your options. If you have any County Court Judgements or other loans or credit outstanding, make arrangements to pay them and tell the bank when you apply for a business bank account. A bank is more likely to look favourably upon your application if you can show you are able and trying to overcome past problems.

Top tip

You might want to ask the following questions when you are window shopping for a business bank account:

→ What is the period of free business banking?

→ What are the charges for paying in cash or cheques?

→ What is the annual charge on a business credit card?

→ How much credit will you give me to start up?

→ Is there a free overdraft facility, and if not, what are the charges?

Making it legal

Before you start trading, you will need to decide on a legal structure for your business, consider the legal implications of what you call your new business and register it with official bodies.

The type of business structure you choose will depend on your own situation. Since it will affect important parts of your business – for example, the amount of tax you pay on your business activities – it's a good idea to get advice from your business adviser or accountant before making a decision.

The three most common legal structures for businesses are:

→ sole trader

→ partnership

→ limited company.

Sole trader

This is the most common way of starting a business and is probably the best option for most first-time entrepreneurs setting up on their own. Sole trader status comes with the easiest legal structure and involves the least paperwork. As a sole trader, you have overall control of your business and will be responsible for any debts the business incurs. You will be regarded as self-employed for tax purposes. This means that you must pay income tax and National Insurance contributions through HM Revenue and Customs' (HMRC) self-assessment system. You will need to register your business with HMRC as soon as you begin to trade. It is free to register, but don't delay, or you may face a penalty charge. (For more on tax, see Four.)

Sole trader

PROS

- Trading is very straightforward - you simply pay tax on your business' profits.
- National Insurance contribution levels are generally lower than those for limited companies.
- This structure has the least amount of paperwork.

CONS

- You are responsible for any money your business owes, such as bank loans for your business' debts. This means you'll have unlimited liability.
- If your business fails, your own assets, such as your home, car or savings could be at risk.
- The amount of money available to sole traders from banks and investors can be limited.
- Some customers and suppliers prefer to deal with limited companies as they are sometimes seen to be more credible.

Partnership

This legal status is used when two or more people want to set up a business together. Like a sole trader, it's easy to register and doesn't involve huge amounts of paperwork. In a partnership, you can have up to 20 partners and the profits from your business will be divided between these partners. Like a sole trader, you will be classed as self-employed for tax purposes and have to pay income tax and National Insurance contributions through the self-assessment system. You'll be responsible for any debts that the business incurs and this responsibility is shared between all the partners.

Before starting a business with other people, it's a good idea to draw up a **Deed of Partnership**, which explains how the partnership will be run. If you don't do this, any disagreements will be ruled by standard laws, which don't take into account your individual circumstances.

Partnership

PROS

- The way you set up a partnership can be flexible and you can set out these arrangements in a Deed of Partnership.
- Responsibilities, risks and losses are shared between several people.
- Partners bring a variety of different skills and experience to the business.
- As more people are involved, you may have access to more money to invest in the business.
- There is less paperwork to deal with compared to a limited company.

CONS

- Like a sole trader, without a separate legal identity the partnership has unlimited liability. This means each partner is personally responsible for the debts of the partnership.
- All the partners can be held responsible for any one partner's negligence. This is important because each partner can make a binding contract without the permission of the others.
- Problems can occur when there are disagreements.

Limited liability partnership

A limited liability partnership (LLP) is similar to a normal partnership, but has the advantage of allowing partners to limit their personal liability. Unlike sole traders and partners of ordinary partnerships, it is the LLP itself, rather than the partners, that is responsible for any debts that it runs up – unless any of the partners have personally guaranteed a loan to the business.

The downside is that LLPs are generally more complicated than ordinary partnerships, as they have to meet many of the same requirements as limited companies, like filing annual accounts at Companies House.

Limited company

A limited company is a separate legal entity (or body) from the people who own the business, unlike a sole trader or a partnership. The main advantage of setting up as a private limited company is that you are not personally responsible for the company's debts. If you're starting a high-risk business that needs a large amount of capital from the start, this option will probably be best. It can also add to credibility and help you look more professional if, for example, you are hoping for good credit terms with suppliers. The downside is that this legal structure is more complex and involves more paperwork and costs.

As a limited company, there must be at least one **shareholder**, at least one **director** and there may also be a **company secretary**. You can have up to 50 shareholders in the company and the liability of each is limited to the value of shares they hold. The company will have to pay **corporation tax** on its total profits – including capital gains – for an accounting period. This is different to sole traders and partnerships, which pay income tax on their profits. The company will need to collect and pay income tax and National Insurance contributions from their employees through a PAYE (Pay As You Earn) system. You will also need to prepare, maintain and submit accounts to Companies House each year. This includes a profit and loss account and balance sheet.

Limited company

PROS
- Your responsibility for debts is limited to the initial cost of your shares.
- Money can be raised by selling shares in the business.
- Employees can own a share of the business.
- A limited company has a legal identity separate from that of its owners – this allows the company to continue trading even if a member resigns or dies.
- The name of the company is protected by law.
- Some suppliers and customers think that limited companies are more credible than other types of businesses.

CONS
- A company has to comply with a lot of complex and detailed legislation, which does not apply to sole traders or partnerships. This can mean more admin and more costs.
- The company's accounts will be publicly available, meaning that anyone can find out how well or badly your company is doing.
- You will often need to give personal guarantees to get bank loans.

Choosing a name

Coming up with a name for your business is a creative and enjoyable process, and can really help you take the first step in realising your ambitions. It's an important part of creating an identity for your business; an identity that will affect who buys from you and who does not.

Our story

Natasha Faith and Semhal Zemikael, La Diosa

We have always been independent, and known that we wanted to start our own businesses. After college we went travelling, looking for inspiration. We went to the Mayan ruins and temples and found a small community in Mexico, who taught us how to make jewellery. It was a great experience, and we fell in love with the concept of big jewellery linked to empowerment. Hence taking the name La Diosa, meaning 'goddess' in Spanish, for our business.

When we first started, we met people in hotels or in clients' homes. It was slightly unprofessional and we wouldn't advise others to do the same, but we had no choice. We could have hired a studio in Stratford, but we needed to reflect our **brand** right from the beginning. If your product is high-end, you need to reflect that with your location. Otherwise you confuse your customer. And it has paid off. Last December we opened a show room in Hatton Garden, the jewellers' heartland, and it is great that clients can come to us directly. We are in a few stockists around the UK (including Harvey Nichols within four months of launching) and will be launching in New York in a few months. Our jewellery has been worn by Sarah Brown, Naomi Campbell and the Duchess of Cornwall.

We want our brand to be a fashion lifestyle brand, all built around the goddess, empowerment theme. Quality, excellence, feeling good, empowerment – these are all things synonymous with the brand. We love designing but ultimately we want to build our brand beyond jewellery. We have already moved into shoes, bikinis, and sunglasses. Hopefully, down the line we will do restaurants and bars. We can always have the dream and idea, and build the strategy around it.

First impressions are important and everyone who interacts with you and your business will form ideas about it based on your business image. Your name will play a large part in establishing what that image is. It therefore has to be something that sits comfortably with the values that you want your business to have.

It's also useful to have a vision for the future in mind. This will help you to come up with a name that will still be appropriate as your business grows and develops. Although it might seem like a good idea to name your business after yourself or the local area, if your aim is to create a national or global brand, the business might grow out of its name.

Do you want a name that will stand out from the crowd? When starting out, cold-calling potential customers and trying to get a minute of their time to explain your business can be an uphill battle. Having a name that sticks in the mind and provokes interest can be a good start or talking point.

Your business name will also need to work well for you on your uniform, stationery, website and marketing materials. An overly complicated or long name may prove tricky to transfer onto a shirt, for example.

'Your brand will be affected by customers' experiences of your business'

My story

Nash Hunter, PC People UK

When I was working as a support engineer, I spotted a gap in the market for supporting business IT systems. The company I was working for collapsed in 2006, so I took the opportunity to set up Banbury PC people.

The name I chose was regional, but I have now taken 'Banbury' out of the company name. We are looking for other companies we can acquire, or business partners who want to do the same as us in other areas, which we would help fund and support for an equity stake. I also want to set up another office around Oxford, so it was right to deregionalise.

The name change has taken around 12 months, and is a very subtle process. We are a young business so we didn't want to do anything that might damage sales leads and enquiries. It started with the way we answer phones, and then we adjusted our headed paper and invoices. It felt wrong to do a big marketing campaign – the softly-softly approach felt better. It didn't knock people's confidence in us, thinking, 'why are they changing?'

My one bit of advice would be to make sure you keep a very close eye on finances and cash flow. You can end up with lots of money outstanding but no cash in the bank, which means you can't do anything. Also analyse your market and the buoyancy of it. It doesn't matter how great your idea is if there is no market for it.

There are regulations that can limit your choice, depending on whether you run your business as a sole trader, partnership or limited company. Whatever type of legal status you choose for your business, you need to follow some golden rules. Your business name cannot:

➔ already be in use by another business

➔ conflict with a registered **trademark**

➔ be offensive

➔ use words restricted by Government – you can find a full list of these words on the Companies House website.

If you choose to run a business using a name that is not your own, you must display the trading name, the individual owner's name or the name of each business partner and the business address on:

➔ your place of business (where you deal with customers and suppliers)

➔ business letters

➔ written orders for goods and services

➔ written demands for payment of business debts.

If you set up a limited company, you must register your business name with Companies House. This isn't necessary for a sole trader or partnership.

Standing out from the crowd

Once you've decided on a name, you may want to design a **logo** for your business. This can convey who you are and what you do in a simple, imaginative and memorable way. Effective logos are unique enough to create a lasting impression on your target market, but simple enough for people to recognise quickly and easily. Your logo must be different from your competitors, and be clear enough to be reproduced to any size and scale, so that it is equally at home on a business card and on a shop front window.

Whatever logo you design for your business, it must not:

→ be in use by another business or be very similar to that of another business

→ conflict with an existing registered trademark

→ be offensive

→ mislead the public

→ constitute a criminal offence – some designs are protected by law such as badges relating to government, national or international institutions (the Olympic Rings, for example).

If you want to use your logo as a trademark you must register it at the Intellectual Property Office (see Six).

'A logo should cover who you are and what you do'

Your business brand

Your company name and logo will play their part in reflecting your business brand, together with the values that you have decided to attach to the business (see One). The important thing about a brand is that it can communicate the heart of your business and what it delivers to your customers. Your brand reflects your business' reputation and its personality – what makes it the business that it is. A powerful brand can demonstrate clearly to your customers why your product or service is different to, and more appealing than, your competitors'.

There are several ways to help people make the link between your brand, your business, and your values; things like smart use of design, advertising and marketing. But ultimately, your brand will be reflected by your customers' experiences of your business – an impression that will be formed with every interaction you have with your customers and suppliers. You need to be sure that you can always live up to your promises, or 'brand values', so think carefully about what your business is good at (i.e. what you can promise) and the values that you have attached to the business. This might include your excellent customer service, the value for money that your product or services provide, or your unique approach.

How much budget you should spend on creating your brand is hard to say, as it should encompass most areas of your business, from stationery, signage and your website, to how you deliver your product or service to customers and time spent training staff. You don't need to do everything at once. The most important thing is that you and your employees understand and can match the expectations set by your brand.

What worked for me

Claire Locke, Artigiano

The important thing about a good brand is that you can command a higher price than your competitors, if people think that it is worth it. An 'also-ran' company producing a generic product can only compete on price, which is something successful businesses just do not do.

A brand name is a promise to the customer. When they hear it, it tells them what to expect, not only in terms of product but price/value relationship, quality, the way in which it will be delivered, and the way they as a customer will be treated. Everything you do, in all areas of your business, must be consistent with your brand values. If you plan to do things to a high quality, you must have your product packaged nicely and talk to customers in a nice, polite way. We encouraged our call centre staff to talk to a customer as much as the customer wanted. When we designed the catalogue for our female clothing range, we wanted to convey that we were top of the market, so we used thick paper and low density photos per page.

There may be temptation or pressure on you to short cut something but you must hold out and stick to your values. There will always be people telling you that you can use cheaper paper, buttons, whatever. You should put yourself in the shoes of the customer, and think, 'how would I feel if I was on the receiving end of this?' If you would mind, you shouldn't be doing it.

Part of branding is what makes you stand out from the rest, so holding those values is critical. I always insisted on having fresh flowers in the entrance hall. Every time we went through budgets, someone would say we could save money there. I would say no way! They are symbolic of the fact that we produce a beautiful catalogue and beautiful clothes in a beautiful environment and we are not having plastic flowers or a dead cactus. Those flowers reminded us of our values every day.

Talk the talk

Sole Trader

The business owner is solely responsible for the running, profits and losses of the business.

Partnership

The partners of the business share with each other the profits or losses of the business.

Limited Liability Company

A separate legal body that can exist in its own right. The company is owned by the shareholders, but the shareholders liability is 'limited' and their personal assets cannot be touched.

Deed of Partnership

A legally binding agreement between the partners who are in business together.

Corporation tax

A tax on the taxable profits of limited companies, including trading and investment profits, and capital gains.

Shareholder

Someone who owns one or more shares in a company.

Director

A member of the board, involved in controlling or directing business development or finances.

Company secretary

The person responsible for making sure that the company meets its statutory obligations (for example, filing accounts with Companies House).

Brand

The image you create for your business including the words and symbols that make up your name, slogan and logo.

Trademark

A legally protected mark or symbol that cannot be copied.

Logo

A combination of characters or graphics that distinguish one business from another.

Budget(ing)

The process of working out what you expect your business to earn and spend within a given period (say, a month or a year).

Personal drawings

Money that you take out of the business as personal wages.

Credit check

A report that all lenders can run on a person applying for finance. The report provides lenders with a picture of your ability to repay finance based on your repayment history.

'Choose your customers'

three

Marketing and sales

Now that you have given your business an identity or brand, you can start planning how you are going to tell people about that brand. That's where good sales and marketing tactics come in. It can be easy to confuse marketing and sales – though the two are closely linked, there are some distinct differences. Simply put, marketing is about leading the horse to water, and sales is about making that horse drink.

Promoting your business to the right people will generate sales and boost your bottom line. But marketing is about more than just finding and getting customers, it's about keeping and developing them too.

Finding and getting the right customers

Trying to sell the same thing to *everybody in the world who might buy from you one day* won't get you very far. Better that you choose your customers – that way you can be certain that your marketing is focused and that you are designing and promoting products and services that your chosen customers, or in other words your **target market**, need.

For example, you may be setting up a karate school. Ask yourself what type of customer fits with your business image.

Our values	Our customers	Business benefit
➜ We believe that self-defence should be accessible and affordable to all children.	➜ We would like to work with schools to offer self-defence classes.	➜ Schools provide regular income.
➜ We believe that children and families need activities they can do together at a competitive price.	➜ We would like to work with families.	➜ Families with children are prepared to spend money on extra-curricular activities.
➜ We care about vulnerable people in the community.	➜ We would like to work with the elderly to teach basic self-defence techniques.	➜ There is little competition in this area. The elderly make referrals.

Once you have identified the core groups that form your target market, you will have a clearer idea of how to communicate with them. If, for example, you can imagine how old they are or where they live, you can imagine what paper or magazine they might read.

Marketing: leading the horse to water

You have your target market in mind. Now you need to tell them you exist and get them knocking on your door, or in other words, get them to come to the water. A great business idea won't succeed unless people know about it. That's where marketing comes in. Often, the simpler and fewer marketing methods you use, the more effective your approach.

Advertising

Advertising is a branded piece of promotion for your business, which you will usually pay to place in a variety of different places; magazines and newspapers, online, TV, radio, cinema, or billboards. Adverts can be seen by a lot of people, but the number of people that will act once they have seen an advert is less than one per cent. However, when adverts work, they can bring in significant income for your business and help to cement your brand in the minds of customers.

Print advertising

Weekly, morning and evening newspapers and magazines can be an effective and cheap way to advertise to your local community. Magazines and newspapers offer lots of different advertising packages, for example:

→ **Classified ads** – these adverts are normally grouped together under a theme and listed alphabetically.

→ **Display and semi-display** – these are bigger (and more expensive), incorporate colour and images and generally appear in the supplements, for example, property or holiday supplements.

→ **Advertisement features** – this is a feature or a story on your business that you pay for, and often includes space for you to advertise.

> **Top tip**
>
> Advertising departments keep media packs that they send out to potential advertisers, listing details on circulation, readership and prices for different types of advert. Ask for a media pack and note that the quoted price for advertising is only a starting point – like anything, you're free to negotiate!

→ **Loose inserts** – these are separate pamphlets inserted into a newspaper or magazine. These are particularly effective if you are promoting a special time-limited offer.

Wherever you place your advert, it will be fighting for attention with many others. Here are some golden rules to help you to stand out from the crowd:

DO

- Make sure your headline is big and bold - use a wide and readable font.
- Get the main point of your message into your headline - four out of five readers never get past that point.
- Tell your customer how you are different from your competitors.
- Keep it simple and get to the point quickly.
- Tell your customer what they need to do - visit a website, cut out a voucher, call a number.
- Make sure your contact details are clear and easy to read.

DON'T

- Let artwork take over - this will cloud the message you're trying to get across.
- Print words across a photo or artwork - your message should be clear to readers and easy to digest in a matter of seconds.
- Leave it to your customer to figure out how they will benefit from your product or service. Tell them.
- Make claims that you can't prove.

Television

TV is a very powerful marketing medium, capable of reaching vast numbers of people when they are paying most attention. It gives you the opportunity to be creative and give the business a personality, but it is probably the most expensive marketing method you can use, and not something you should do without thinking very carefully.

Radio

Radio advertising can be a cheaper alternative to TV advertising and can be particularly effective if you choose a slot carefully, like a 'rush hour' slot when people are travelling to and from work. On the downside, a radio ad can't be cut out and kept like a printed advert nor will it leave an image with a listener – the saying 'a picture is worth a thousand words' is often true.

Publicity – hold the front page

Anyone with money to throw at promoting their business can advertise, but you can maximise exposure and boost your sales for free if you know how to work the media.

Publicity is about getting media coverage – whether in newspapers, magazines, radio or TV – for your business without having to pay for costly advertising space. Free publicity sounds great, but you can waste a lot of time and energy making phone calls and drafting **press releases** that never result in any media coverage. Following a few simple steps will help:

Top tip

The national media often picks up on stories that break first in the local media and trade press so focus your energy on building good relationships with local journalists first.

➜ **Target audience** – remind yourself of your target market and which media they are most likely to use.

➜ **What's the story** – brainstorm all of the interesting stories there are to tell about your business: is there an event, something controversial, a survey, research and statistics, or a human interest story you could use to capture the attention of the media? There might be an interesting story behind your business name, how you have succeeded against the odds, or how a customer has used your product in an unusual way.

➜ **Playing the game** – be prepared to be persistent and persuasive – not pushy – to win media coverage. Do your homework; know what story you intend to pitch, and any information you need to back it up, know the particular media inside out, and follow up your press release with a phone call.

➜ **Prepare** – know what you're going to say and make a note of the key points that you want to get across.

➜ **Select your target** – pick the right person to pitch to and make the phone call at an appropriate time – for example, not when a paper is going to press or when a radio show is on air. Some papers and magazines have a **features schedule** that will help you to identify the best time to submit your story and to tell the editor which feature you think it would suit.

Cut out the middleman?

Direct marketing is a form of advertising where a business can reach its audience without using the normal channels listed earlier in the chapter, like radio and newspapers. Instead, businesses communicate directly with the customer, using direct mail, leaflet drops, SMS texting, the internet and so on.

The great thing about a well-planned direct marketing campaign is that it can be measured easily. Customers can be encouraged to respond – for example, a poster carrying a phone number or a leaflet with a reply box. If you send 1,000 leaflets and receive 100 answers, you can say you had a 10 per cent response rate. You can divide your target audience into key sectors, for example, age, gender or occupation, and record their responses to your promotion by the hour, day, week or month.

'Marketing is about more than just finding customers, it's about keeping them too'

DIRECT MARKETING DOs

- Get your timing right – for example, if you're reminding parents that their children will need new school uniforms for the new term, then you will need to make contact over the summer months.
- Consider offering an incentive like a special offer or a discount for responses to your campaign.
- Save money by getting in on someone else's direct marketing campaign – for example, catalogues, featuring in the menu of a new local restaurant.
- Get a relevant mailing list – you can source detailed mailing lists for both businesses and consumers from some commercial providers on the Direct Marketing Association website.
- Code every piece of marketing material you produce for your direct marketing campaign so that you can find out which generates the most interest and sales.

DIRECT MARKETING DON'Ts

• Start a direct marketing campaign if you don't have the staff to cope with extra orders.

• Make contact with people who have ticked a box to say they don't want to receive such communications. People can register their preferences with central registers so it's important that you check your contact list against these central registers first. You should check:

- the Fax Preference Service (FPS)
- the Telephone Preference Service (TPS)
- the E-mail Preference Service (EPS)
- the Mailing Preference Service (MPS).

• You will need to pay to subscribe to view these lists.

Leaflets

Leaflet drops are a very simple and cheap means of direct marketing and can be effective if you are a local business providing a local service, such as a taxi, food delivery or mobile hairdressing service. But most leaflets end up in the bin – so what's different about the ones that result in sales?

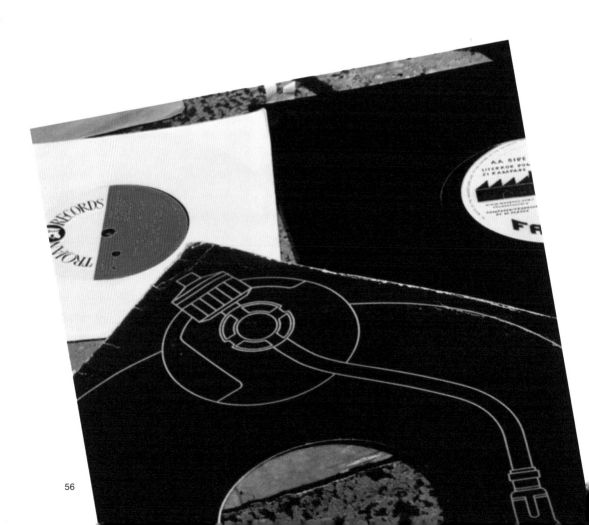

DO

- Think of your leaflet as an advert and apply the same golden rules – have an attention-grabbing headline, a reason to keep reading, and an easy and immediate means of making contact.
- Give your leaflet to somebody who will check it for errors and give you honest feedback.
- Think about the format – a reader's eye will flow over the leaflet starting from the top left hand corner to the right bottom corner. The top left corner and bottom right corner are 'hot spots' so make use of them.
- Include 'buzz words' – put yourself in your customer's shoes; we all like words like 'Free', 'Bonus', 'Exclusive', 'New', 'Save'.
- Make sure that any offers you include are time-limited.

DON'T

- Waste space – use both sides of the leaflet. If a leaflet lands face down on a customer's doormat, it's no better than scrap paper!
- Put your business name at the top of your leaflet – customers aren't interested in your business name, only what you can offer them.
- Print thousands of leaflets – they will quickly go out of date.
- Pack your leaflet full of text – all you need is a headline, a clear message and a call to action.
- Use long sentences – less is definitely more!
- List the _features_ of your product or service, tell customers about the _benefits_ instead – most customers don't care about the features of a lawnmower for example, but they do want to know whether they can store it easily in their shed and how quickly it will get the job done!

My story

Lucy Mann, Nine Months

I always knew I wanted to run my own business. When I had twin boys, I found that there weren't many places I could go to buy a pushchair or buy nice gifts, and that's when I thought about a nursery shop. I had worked in the promotions department at Galaxy Radio when it was first launching in the North East. We promoted the station while the test transmissions were happening. I learnt so much about building up brand awareness from nothing. The marketing department was the biggest department at the station, and I saw it all. I thought of the name of the shop, Nine Months, when working at Galaxy, and bought the domain name off the internet.

But I realised if I was going to start my own business, I needed to know how a smaller business worked, so I went to work as a PA at a hairdressers for a while, to understand staffing and general business stuff.

When Nine Months first opened, I got good press coverage through The Prince's Trust because I was a good story – a single mum running her own business.

We sent out flyers and did a mailshot to private nurseries and toddler groups in the area, which was probably our biggest marketing success. I sat with a pile of envelopes and money-off vouchers and 300 second-class stamps. Ads in local glossy magazines were good too. Hairdressers keep them and they are not thrown away so quickly.

But there's no point in advertising if you haven't got a brand. You can build up a brand reputation with badges, car stickers, comp slips, letterheads and external branding. I learnt from Galaxy that the important thing is keeping things similar, and getting that continuity.

Sales promotions

You may want to consider offering your target market a sales promotion or an incentive to buy your product or service. Some of the most popular are:

→ **Money-off coupons** – coupons that customers can cut out of a newspaper or product packaging to receive a discount next time they buy. These are normally used by customers who already buy the relevant product or service – they are not particularly effective at attracting new customers.

→ **Competitions** – where buying the product will allow the customer to enter a competition or where the customer enters a competition to win, for example, the first in a series of books or a magazine subscription.

→ **Demonstrations** – a great way of attracting attention with a lively display, although they can be expensive to run.

→ **Discount vouchers** – a popular way of promoting a new menu at a restaurant or a typically quiet period for theme parks or restaurants.

→ **Free gifts** – rewarding purchases over a set amount with a free gift.

→ **Loyalty cards** – a popular way of rewarding returning customers by allowing them to collect points they can use in store, to win prizes or access special offers.

→ **Point of sales promotions** – an effective way of promoting, for example, a new or a seasonal product with attractive displays or posters at till points or on your website homepage.

→ **Samples** – these can help potential customers get a feel for your product or service, but can be expensive.

The most important thing to remember when planning a sales promotion is that you calculate how many extra sales you will need to make to cover the cost of your promotion.

Take your message online

Don't make the mistake of creating a website just to follow the crowd – be clear in your own mind why you might need one. Return to your market research: do your potential customers currently buy your product or service online? Are your potential customers likely to shop online in the future? Is there an opportunity for your business to change the way customers currently buy your product or service – for example, do they currently buy on the high street but in future would buy online? If you can answer 'yes' to one or all of these questions, the chances are your business should have a professional website.

Businesses of all shapes and sizes may have a website, but not all will be designed to meet their needs or the needs of their customers. Spend time thinking about what you would like your website to achieve:

→ to increase sales by creating an online shop and allowing customers to buy online

→ to attract more customers by having a professional presence online

→ to increase awareness of your brand and raise your profile

→ to have a campaigning tool that will allow customers to debate, read press cuttings and be involved in promotional activities

→ to lower costs by reducing the overheads of your business – for example, rent

→ to encourage interaction and feedback from your customers.

Your business brand will need to work as well on your website as in other areas of your business. A web designer or web design agency can help you to do this through use of design, colour and fonts; you will get a professional website, but for a professional fee.

If you don't need a high specification website, you might want to explore cheaper software packages that make it easy for you to build your own website.

Once you are familiar with the web, there are a few things that you might want to consider experimenting with.

Pay-Per-Click advertising

Pay-Per-Click advertising (PPC) is a popular way of advertising online and means that your advert will get exposure on search engines such as Google and associated websites. Pay-Per-Click advertising does what it says on the tin; you pay when someone clicks on your advert. There are a number of networks that offer PPC advertising, so shop around and test out some different ones.

Cost-per-thousand advertising

Cost-Per-Thousand or Cost-Per-Mile advertising (CPM) means that you pay for adverts upfront. You might choose to pay for one thousand 'impressions,' which means that your advert will appear one thousand times on relevant websites.

If you're thinking of running a web marketing campaign, it's worth comparing your best quotes for both PPC and CPM advertising and compare the cost per click with the cost per number of impressions.

Blogging and Twitter

A blog is just an online journal – an internet user posting text about a particular topic or theme – that can be accessed by other internet users who want to keep up to date with new entries. A blog can 'link' to another blog whose topic is similar or complementary. You can use a blog to start a debate about a new product, comment on research associated with your market or to introduce special offers and events – all in a creative and informal way.

If you fancy trying your hand at blogging, here are some things to keep in mind:

➔ **Keep your blog reader-friendly** – write as you would speak to your customers and let as much of your personality as possible shine through.

➔ **Don't make your blog too specific** – not only will you struggle to come up with varied and interesting content, but your readers will struggle to comment.

➔ **Make updates** – little, high quality and often.

➔ **Don't promote your link all over the web** – you'll be seen as a spammer and it'll reduce the likelihood of other blogs linking to your blog.

Twitter works in a similar way to a blog. It allows you to put a face on your business; one that has people behind it, travelling to work, and working in offices. Customers can keep 'up-to-the-minute' with your business if, for example, you have some breaking news, and can see that you are active in the same spaces that they are. If you're thinking of tweeting about your business, it's worth checking out any existing mentions of your business and your competitors – following others 'tweeting' first will give you a feel for the media.

Social networking

Most people are familiar with Facebook, one of the most popular social networking sites. But there are now social networking sites designed specifically to help small businesses develop an online presence, network and share information – BT Tradespace for example. Businesses can upload a profile, photos, blog and maps quickly, and for free. With sites like this, LinkedIn and, of course, Facebook, it's very easy to make contacts and build an online community that will benefit your business.

If you're planning on using social networking to promote your business, here are some tips:

 Research which social networking sites suit your business needs and be selective – for making contacts and networking professionally, LinkedIn or Facebook might be your best options. But if you're a musician, then MySpace should be your first call.

➔ Be active – update content regularly and encourage others with similar interests to interact with your content.

➔ Keep your personal social networking profile completely separate from your professional social networking profile.

YouTube

YouTube sometimes gets a bad press but there are lots of creative ways it can be used to generate positive interest in your business. YouTube can help you to turn the spotlight on a particular campaign you are running, introduce a new product or area of your business, or give customers an 'inside view' of your business. You could, for example, give them a virtual tour of your office. You could also improve your reputation for customer care by, for example, sharing recipes if you are a restaurant. Always be careful to protect your personal data and don't show your name, home address or contact details. Also, make sure that you understand YouTube's copyright policy.

'You can maximise exposure and boost sales if you know how to work the media'

What worked for me

James Caan, Hamilton Bradshaw

Marketing is a critical component of any business. You can only sell a service if people know about it. It doesn't matter how good or creative your product or service may be, if it is not communicated or marketed effectively, you don't have a business.

Credit: Joel Anderson

No one kind of method is better than the rest. Dip your toe in until you find the one that is most suitable. But even then, there are no guarantees. I have had marketing campaigns that didn't work, things that generated less activity than it took me to run the campaign. However, you should be able to monitor each campaign very effectively, and track the responses. Remember that sometimes volume isn't the answer – it's customers you need, not enquiries. A good measure of customer service is how much repeat business you get. If people don't come back, clearly there is a message there. You should encourage feedback. Call your customers and check to see if what you are offering is actually being delivered. The better you understand your customers, the better able you are to serve them. Always take their details when they come in and stay in touch with them. It's not difficult to ask for a business card or an email address. Better to ask for their details and be turned down than not to ask at all. And if you are not doing it, someone else is.

To engage with them, there are various effective methods available today. In the current market, one of the best marketing methods is social media, as it is the most cost-effective means of communication. We find LinkedIn very effective, very powerful and it's free. Twitter is also useful for communicating things and events we are doing. You can use Twitter to point people in a certain direction, to a web site, event or specific activity. If you are a recruitment agency and have a position, you can announce it and tell people to go to the web page for further information. It's immediate, cost-effective and easy to do.

Yet the best marketing tip I was ever given was to pick up the phone – as simple as that. It's amazing that people don't do it more and it's probably because of the fear of rejection. I'd say get over that and think that the more 'no's' you get, the closer you are to a 'yes'. If you are afraid of the first no, you will never get to a 'yes'.

Sales: making the horse drink

Selling is the key to a profitable business – it's as simple as that. Once you have got people to your shop or interested in your business, if they won't put their hands in their pockets, there will be no money to keep your business going. The word 'selling' might make you shudder with nerves – we can't all be born salespeople – but you will need to conquer any nerves and develop this skill if your business is to do well.

You don't have to be a 'wheeler-dealer', or blessed with 'the gift of the gab' to sell: in fact, it's often better if you're not. All of us at some point in our lives, with or without knowing, have had experience of selling and being sold to. Have you ever:

→ met and chatted to a stranger who became your friend?

→ persuaded a friend to see your choice of film in the cinema?

→ gone on a first date and found that you have common ground?

→ attended a job interview and got the job?

→ persuaded someone to see and perhaps adopt your point of view?

We may not think of ourselves as salespeople but all of us, without fail, sell to people day in, day out, and think nothing of it.

Selling is a two-way street and isn't just about the person doing the selling. Put yourself in the buyer's shoes. Knowing what a buyer will need from you in order to make a purchase will help you to plan what you are going to say.

When you focus on the buyer rather than on your worries as a seller, you can begin to think of selling as sharing information or benefits or even as sharing your enthusiasm and passion for something. You don't have to call it 'selling'. Call it by another name that helps you to think of the process in a more authentic and natural way and you may find that your confidence rockets!

The golden rules of selling

A lot of time and money is invested in developing sales training but really all you need to know are a few 'must-dos'.

People buy people

People are more likely to buy from a person with whom they have a rapport. Think of your body language and remember to smile, be enthusiastic and keep eye contact (without staring!).

Sell the benefits

Customers need to buy solutions to their problems, so find the problem and sell the solution. When you talk to customers, ask the right questions and listen to what they are saying to find out what they need.

Recognise the buying signals

Look out for signs that the customer is ready to buy. Clues might be if they are looking at one particular product and asking detailed questions, or asking you for a second opinion. Don't continue selling when you have seen these signs. Move onto asking questions like, 'So do you think he would prefer the black or the grey?'.

Follow up

This is just as important as the sale itself. Think about your conversation and ask yourself what you learned about the customer that might be useful, either for future sales (what are their future plans, for example) or for building relations (do they have children, for example).

So they said no — this time!

You may get several no's before getting a sale; don't be put off! 'No' simply means that the product you're selling is not right for them at that time. Don't be afraid to ask why the customer decided against it. The answer might be surprising and might even end up in the sale you thought you'd lost.

Bounce back

Keep in touch with the customer if that's possible, and if you say you'll follow up, make sure you do. And above all stay motivated. We all know knock-backs aren't personal, but it can start to feel that way if you don't take time to prepare yourself for the next call.

'Selling is a two-way street'

Events – trade shows and exhibitions

Trade shows and exhibitions have a reputation for bringing together businesses and customers who have a common interest – for example, The Ideal Home Show brings together businesses and customers who are interested in home interiors and gardens. To find out whether a particular show will benefit your business, ask the organisers:

→ **Who are the key exhibitors and media partner for the show** – these will reflect the show's target audience and you can judge whether this is the right target market for your business.

→ **What were the show sales figures from the previous year** – this is a more important statistic than visitor numbers because it shows you the number of people who were willing to part with their cash.

→ **What were the media coverage statistics from the previous year** – this will help you to judge whether the show will get coverage in media that will reach your target market.

My story

Matthew Harris, Joseph Lamsin jewellery

I worked for a jewellery firm when I left school, but I was frustrated by the lack of freedom. My creativity and ideas weren't being used. I thought if I had my own business I could do what I want.

Initially I took on commissions for friends and family, but I was developing my own style. I wanted to give people the best level of service possible, and to build a brand with set values, which would reflect my background and the things that inspired me. I didn't want to produce jewellery that looked mass-produced. I wanted it to be personal and have a story behind it that people could connect to.

Within a year I had to drastically change things. I had been hand-making bespoke pieces using labour-intensive methods that made my pricing out. Now I use outside firms for some of the processes, but I wasted a lot of money and time, and better research of customers and competitors would have sussed that out. I also did a big trade show that was poorly attended, which was another waste of money and time. Talking to people is good. I was shy of asking jewellers their opinion, as I thought they would see me as competition. But people are more than happy to talk about their business. I even had a successful London jeweller tell me who it uses for polishing work, which is a key part of its business.

I know that now I need to get my website optimised to get more traffic, and to concentrate on PR and getting my products seen and my name out there. I am trying to juggle things and work out where best to invest. My mentors have really helped. When I don't know what to do next, they will break it down and make it much clearer.

Having my own business and doing what I love doing makes living worthwhile. It's not all about money. As long as you are comfortable, doing something you enjoy is much more important.

Keeping the customer

There is no secret formula for good customer service. We all know what contributes to whether we have a good experience or a bad experience in, for example, a high street shop, and we all know how important it is. It boils down to whether we leave feeling valued; could we find someone to help us, were they willing and keen to help, was it easy for us to part with our money and did we get good value for our money?

The basics of good customer service couldn't be easier:

→ Provide a good quality product or service that is value for money.

→ Put the customer first and go out of your way to help. If for example, stock isn't available on the shelf, can it be found elsewhere?

→ Be polite and friendly to customers and build up a good rapport that encourages them to return to your business.

→ Resolve complaints quickly and politely and don't try and pass the buck. Build trust between you and your customer.

→ Ask for and use feedback constructively.

There are several ways you can start to build a reputation for good customer service within your business. Here are just some to get you started:

➜ **Customer service guarantee** – create a customer service policy and make sure that everyone in the business understands and works to the policy. Display it somewhere your customers can see it. Your policy might promise, for example, free delivery or a 30 day money-back guarantee – whatever you promise, make sure you can achieve it. You can promise to respond to a complaint or feedback within 10 working days, but what does promising 'a speedy service' mean?

➜ **Customer feedback** – make it easy for your customers to give feedback and let them know how you plan to use it.

➜ **Complaints** – never be afraid of complaints: they are an opportunity to put things right or *better* than they were before, and we often learn more from the things we do wrong than the things we do right. If a customer complains in person, take them somewhere quiet, remain calm and polite and concentrate on how you fix the problem.

Once you've got the basics, you'll soon be able to start promoting your business, mastering your sales technique and making sure that your customers keep coming back for more.

Talk the talk

Target market

The market you have identified as having the most need for your product or service.

Press release

A written or recorded announcement to the media requesting coverage of a newsworthy story or event.

Features schedule

A timetable of stories that a newspaper or magazine will run, which helps journalists and advertisers with forward planning.

'No matter
how brilliant
your business,
without cash it
will fail'

four

Managing your money

The success of your business will depend on your ability to make money. No matter how brilliant you and your business are, without cash, the business will fail. Time and again, successful business people will tell you that the single most important tip is to watch your cash and make sure there is always money in the bank. Without money you can't make products, or pay bills, suppliers or staff.

Your money

Some of us have always overspent before payday arrives; others are born savers, good at squirreling away money for a rainy day. But whatever your natural tendency, it's a good idea to work out exactly how much money you need to survive, and therefore how much you will need your business to make. This could help you judge whether your business idea will work for you.

Your survival income is the minimum amount of money you need to take from the business to maintain your standard of living, and to cover costs such as tax and National Insurance contributions. It's important to still include money you will need to meet up with friends and live a normal life – you need to keep a balance between home and work, while being realistic about how much hard work will be needed at first.

It may be some months before your business starts to make money, so make sure your **personal survival budget** is realistic, in order that you can identify where you can make savings in your personal spending. That will mean you can commit more money to supporting your business.

What worked for me

Tim Roupell, The Daily Bread

When I set up my business, I had spent 10 years working for other people and I was terrified of going back to that. Having no money behind me, the business needed to make a profit almost from day one and I was absolutely determined it would succeed, so counting the pennies was critical.

I drew up a kind of personal survival budget. I knew that I needed £200 a week to live, so that was what I needed to earn. In the hope that I would make about 50p profit per sandwich, that meant I had to sell 400 sandwiches a week – it was a back of a fag packet calculation, but worth doing. This obsession with controlling costs and concentrating on bottom line net profit remained with me for the remaining 23 years that I ran the company. I had to make a success of it, and it had to provide enough money for me to live off, and if there was a gap in sales, I didn't know how I was going to survive.

Cash flow is everything. Pretty successful businesses with a good model can still go bust because of a lack of cash. You have to count every penny and challenge every expense.

One of the ironies of developing a business is that the more you are growing, the more cash you need to have in your business. You can easily move from getting cash in hand from small clients to dealing with larger companies who pay on 90 days. We were very focused on chasing payments and kept money in the business. I paid myself what I needed to live and kept the rest in the business in case it was needed.

Be wary of growing too fast and taking on staff before you can afford them, and accept that you are going to have to work incredibly hard to get the business off the ground. The first few years will be the hardest as you try and develop momentum and build up sales, and there will inevitably be mistakes made as you find your way. Mistakes are fine, just so long as you learn from them and don't repeat them. When you do get help, employ the best people you can and really look after the outstanding ones – you won't grow the business without them by your side.

We were also careful not to have an account that was more than 25 per cent of the business. At one point we had a client that accounted for 33 per cent of our sales and that was terrifying and we felt far too vulnerable to them. Our solution was to pull out all the stops to build up other business, thereby diluting them. Credit risk is also an important area and the rule is pretty simple – if you are at all worried that you might not get paid, then don't deal with someone. We often turned away large sales opportunities for this reason. Also, make sure you always make a reasonable margin on any new business. Too many companies get lured by the promise of huge volume, and discount their prices to win the business only to find that they are making a loss.

When the time comes, make sure you employ people with complementary skills to your own. Being on top of your financial position is critical and if money isn't your strong point, ask questions, listen, and take advice. It is essential to have a good bookkeeper, and if you can't do it (and I wouldn't blame you if you can't) then you must find someone who can. It doesn't matter how passionate you are about your product or service – if it isn't making money, then you're not going to be doing it for very long. Nothing is more important than being on top of your numbers.

Otherwise, keep everything as simple as you can at all times, keep positive, and try as much as you can to enjoy the ride.

Record keeping

Money doesn't take care of itself. You will need to keep track of everything coming in and going out of your business, and that means keeping good records. With accurate records, you can keep track of both your income and expenses, and so understand how well your business is doing. You will also have the necessary records for filing your tax return to HMRC.

There are various methods of record keeping and you will need to choose one that best suits your business. If your business buys and sells products and services using cash only, you will simply need a cash book to keep records of the cash that comes in and goes out. If you start paying for products and services on account, or have to wait before being paid by your customers, you will need to add sales and purchase ledgers to your record keeping system. A **sales ledger** records the sales your business has made so far, the amount of money you have received for your product or services, and the money still owed at the end of each month by customers who are yet to pay.

It's useful because it helps you to keep track of slow payers who you can then chase, and also see which customers are most profitable. A **purchase ledger** works in a similar way for your purchases. It will show all the purchases you have made, and how much you still owe at any one time.

The cash book

A cash book is the business owner's bible. It's where you will record all the money coming in and going out of your business and it's key for recording what happens day-to-day in your business, and for showing how much money you have at any one time.

You can buy a cash book from any stationery retailer or complete a cash book online using a simple spreadsheet or software programme. We've included a sample page from a typical cash book, which generally includes the following information:

→ **incomings and outgoings** – money coming into and going out of your business is recorded separately

→ **date** – the date the transaction took place

→ **details of the transaction** – details of what was bought or sold and to whom

→ **reference** – the type of transaction that took place – for example, cash, cheque or card plus an identifying number

→ **total cost** – the total amount of money paid in and paid out of your business.

You may choose to update your cash book every day (although there is no set time limit); that way you can make sure that nothing gets forgotten or left to the last minute when you come to file your annual tax return.

By law, you'll need to keep all the information about your business' financial transactions for six years. This includes records of all money paid in and taken from the business, bank statements and cheque book stubs.

Cash flow

Your cash book will show what actually happens from month to month in terms of money coming in and going out of your business. This movement of money is called cash flow. Money will not necessarily come into the business at the same time as you need to pay your costs. If the 'flow' of money coming in is more than you are paying out, you will have surplus cash in the business. If you are having problems getting paid, or are not paid regularly, you may struggle to pay your bills when you have to.

The money flowing in and out of your business month by month, throughout the year, can be recorded in a separate document, also called a cash flow. This document will allow you to look back at past months and analyse whether your business is bringing in more than it is paying out. It can also show where the peaks and troughs are in your business income and expenditure. For example, if you're a florist, it can show whether you have higher income in December in preparation for Christmas, and lower income during quieter months like January. This means that it can be used to help you plan for the following year - showing you, for example, when you can afford to spend more because you're likely to have a busy month and when you should keep money in the business because you're likely to have a quiet month.

Cash flow forecast

Working out your cash flow will help you more accurately predict when your business is likely to have a poor month. Armed with this information, you can draw up a cash flow forecast. This is a prediction of what income and expenditure you're likely to have over a forthcoming year, and will help you plan ahead.

'Cash is king'

It can be difficult to complete a cash flow forecast for your first year of trading. Once you have been in business for a while, you will be able to look at sales and costs from the previous year to predict what might happen in the next year. When you first start out, the simplest way is to:

→ List all the amounts of cash you expect the business to receive in (for example, sales) and pay out (for example, rent, bills and wages) in the next 12 months.

→ Predict when each amount of cash will be received or paid – and try to be as realistic as possible. Think about whether the cash will be received or paid in one lump sum or whether it will arrive evenly over a number of months.

→ In a table, enter the cash amounts in the columns month by month – for example, if you run a florist or toy shop you may be able to predict a higher amount of cash coming into your business over the Christmas period, or if you rent business premises, you will be able to enter your monthly rent in each column over a 12-month period.

→ Add in the opening bank balance. If you're about to start your business, for example, your opening balance will be your start-up finance, such as a business loan or grant.

→ For each month, add the opening bank balance plus the total cash your business received and minus the total cash your business paid out to give you the closing bank balance.

→ The closing bank balance for the month then becomes the opening bank balance for the next month.

Break-even

Your break-even point is the level of sales you need to make to cover the costs of running your business. It's the point at which your business is making neither a profit nor a loss – meaning the business isn't generating income for you.

Working out your break-even point should be something you do regularly because it's a figure that will change over time – for example, your suppliers may choose to increase their prices or your rent may increase, which will have an impact on what it costs you to run your business. To do this, you will need to know:

➔ **fixed costs** of running your business – costs to your business that don't change regardless of whether your sales go up or down, e.g. rent, heating, insurance

➔ **variable costs** of running your business – costs that go up and down as a result of the number of sales of your product or service, e.g. raw materials, or costs of transportation.

My story

Michelle Myers, Eco-Kids

The first year was awful. There were so many times I wished I could jack it in. I was planning sessions, doing adverts and leaflet drops, trying to learn about the finances, designing the website, and I was running before I could walk. I thought it would be sunshine and flowers, but it just didn't stop.

I spent loads of money on equipment, decoration and advertising – now we rarely do advertising. I rented premises that didn't have toilets so I had them installed, which came to £1600. My budget was only £4000. I literally had nothing left from day one. I couldn't afford to pay myself and didn't have a good handle on what I was paying out and what was coming in. I was so focused on everything being perfect, and didn't listen when people said, 'Why do you need premises? Just go into a church hall for an afternoon. Keep some money back.' I lumbered myself with huge overheads from the start, which put my business back by one year. If I had my time again, I would do everything differently.

The start was very challenging but now two years on, it is exciting. Our eco kids clubs, centred around eco craft, gardening and cookery, are run by three members of staff. And I have a business partner who is great. While I am on the inventive, creative side, she is more administrative and handles invoices, although we also use local accountants. They are trainees at the local college who do it for £10/month. We just send in receipts and they do everything including cash analysis, and cash flow. Their teacher oversees everything – it's brilliant!

For the next stage, I am thinking about ad deals for our website, an organic cotton clothing range, and branded garden and cooking equipment. We have started a franchise model, and my aim is to have 100 franchises, within three–five years. Then I'll move onto my next thing. I'll be on Dragons' Den soon, but not as an entrant. I'll be on the panel!

Getting paid

Sometimes getting paid is harder than it sounds. If you're selling directly to the public, you'll probably be paid as soon as your product or service changes hands. You may be dealing with debit and credit cards which require you to have specific equipment to process transactions. If you're selling to other businesses, you'll be using an invoicing system, which makes getting paid a more complicated process.

'Money doesn't take care of itself'

Invoicing

An invoice is a formal record of trading between you and your customers. It is used as the basis for all financial management and accounting processes in a business, and is a key document in your tax records. It is also important to your customers, because it acts as their proof of purchase, particularly if you give your customers credit (allow them to delay paying), when the invoice becomes a debt to the business.

You should issue an invoice for each transaction in which your business supplies products or services to a customer and is yet to receive payment for those products and services. Remember to include on the invoice:

Top tip

Check every line of invoices you receive from suppliers. Your suppliers won't necessarily tell you about price hikes – you'll have to spot those yourself!

➔ a unique invoice number

➔ date of the invoice

➔ your business name, address and telephone number

➔ details about the products or services you've supplied – for example, what was bought and how much was charged

➔ your registration number – if you're a limited company

➔ your VAT number – if your business is registered for VAT

➔ your payment terms – the date you want to receive the money, for example, 'invoice payable 30 days from the date of issue'.

Businesses usually allow other businesses more time to pay, although you'll find that your suppliers will demand immediate payment until they trust you to pay on time. You may also want to agree favourable payment terms to a business that has become a long-standing customer.

Chasing late payments

Late payments cause all businesses problems, but the impact is often worse for a small business. Problems arise when a business has a large amount of forecast income – income that it is expecting to receive – but does not receive that income until months later. This means that planning for expenditure in these months can be difficult.

Here are some tips to help you chase invoices and get paid on time:

→ **Ask customers for a reference code** – your customer may be able to provide you with a Purchase Order number to note on the invoice. They may have approved expenditure against this reference code, in which case it will be easier to pay your invoice.

→ **Set up shorter payment terms** – setting up a time frame of 14 days will make customers recognise that they need to settle your invoice sooner than other invoices they receive.

→ **For particular businesses agree a deposit** – for businesses working in some sectors, or on big projects, it would be a good idea to agree 50 per cent payment up front, followed by a second payment on completion.

→ **Offer customers a number of payment options** – allowing your customers to pay by BACS, CHAPS (forms of electronic transfer) and cheques makes it easier for them to pay on time or at short notice.

→ **Include your details on the invoice** – this will help your customer to record you quickly and simply on their purchasing systems. Including bank details will help with BACS or CHAPS payments.

→ **Chase customers a week before payment is due** – payments can fall behind because an invoice has missed a company's payment slot (if say, payments are made weekly).

→ **Call customers the day payment is due** – don't be afraid to call customers the day an invoice is due to be paid for a friendly reminder. If customers assure you the cheque is in the post, make sure you agree a time when you will call back to check on progress.

→ **Offer an incentive for early payment** – consider offering preferential rates or a discount to customers for early payment.

→ **Draw on the big guns** – if all your attempts at chasing have prompted no response, then send a letter that threatens legal action and be sure to keep copies of all your correspondence.

As a last resort, don't be afraid to take legal action:

→ You can use the County Courts and the small claims procedure for debts owed that come to less than £5,000.

→ You can ask a solicitor to chase the debt for you – this will be expensive and is only worthwhile for recovering large debts.

→ You can hire a debt collection agency, which will charge a fee for chasing the amount.

Annual accounts

Regular record keeping of the money coming in and going out of your business will mean that you have all the evidence you need to complete your annual accounts. Sole traders and most partnerships don't need to submit formal accounts, but must complete a self-assessment tax return and send this to HMRC. However, if you are looking for a loan or mortgage to grow your business, most lenders will want to see three years' accounts. A limited company, as it is a more complex legal structure, will need to complete annual accounts to send to HMRC, Companies House and its shareholders.

Preparing your annual accounts or tax return shouldn't be difficult if you keep your cash book up to date through the year. It's a good time to think carefully about your business and take a step back from all that has gone on in the past year. You will be able to take a look at your performance over a full year and pick out where you can increase profit or cut costs, and importantly, where there might be opportunities.

'Sales on paper don't add up to much if people haven't paid you'

Hiring an accountant

It's tempting to think that you can do all this work yourself and save costs, but many businesses prefer to turn to an accountant for at least some of it. If numbers are not your strength, it may be better for you to get professional help so that you can spend more of your time running the business and concentrating on what you are good at. An accountant will be able to do certain things more efficiently than you, because of his expertise.

If you decide to use an accountant, make sure that you find one best suited to your business. As well as confirming charges and what is covered, check whether they have clients both in your sector and of a similar size. Also, it's worth asking who will actually do the work, and what additional services they may be able to offer as and when your business grows.

Our story

Claire Van Looy and Kate Trussell, Teme Valley Care

Our business provides care services for the elderly and disabled. We started out with just Kate and me, and for a year we were working seven days a week, and nights. Now we have 26 staff and are based in a three-storey office. And we have an accountant god love him! If I set up again, I would have an accountant from the word go. At the time I thought, 'It can't be that hard.' We had set the business up ourselves, but as much as you can read up, you can't know all the loopholes and ins and outs, or the best way of dealing with things. It was horrendous at first and we paid tax we shouldn't have. I just didn't realise accountants could be so affordable, and you can pay by monthly direct debit. We still know about everything coming in and going out, but they do our payslips, tax and self-assessment. We haven't got the time for it with 26 staff. I just had a call about a lady dying of cancer, so I will have to juggle the rotas to make sure we can put in care instantly for her last days. I can't be thinking about payslips.

Cash flow has got harder, the bigger we have got. We will probably need someone to come in full time. We used to just have private clients who would pay on day one, but now we do a lot of work for the NHS and social services. They pay 30 days from date of invoice, so we are always a month behind. I have to keep on their case chasing payments, and finance takes up most of my time. But it is so rewarding. We all know someone with problems who needs support at home. That is what we are here for.

Controlling costs

Reviewing your annual accounts will help you to look at ways you can control costs to boost your profit. It's a good idea to have a 'make do and mend' approach when you first start out. You might always have had in mind to have your own office, for example, but would it better to share with someone else and halve the cost? Or offer a free sample of your product or service in return for free advertising? Start by looking at the areas where you have the highest costs. Some areas you could look at might be:

➜ **Banking** – keep tabs on the sort of transactions you're processing (e.g. cash, credit or cheque) and ensure that you have business banking that gives favourable rates on the transactions you process. Try to stay in credit and so avoid paying fees.

➜ **Stock costs** – find suppliers that are competitive and efficient.

➜ **Sales and marketing** – consider whether you can cut out any marketing costs that aren't generating sales.

➜ **Telephone bills** – consider whether you could use e-mail for some communications or whether you can shop around for another provider.

➜ **Utility bills** – think about how you could cut down your supplies, for example, a florist may be able to install a water butt that will collect rainwater for keeping flowers.

➜ **Postage and stationery** – could some correspondence be sent by second class post?

➜ **Travel** – think about whether you can plan travel in advance to benefit from cheaper fares.

➜ **Wages** – could fewer people do the same job? Is using volunteers or interns an option?

Stock control

Stock control is a system of responding to orders in the most efficient way and another good place to make savings. Good stock control is all about having enough of the right stock in the right place at the right time. It means that you can:

→ always supply your customers without tying up too much money in stock

→ know how much to order and anticipate seasonal or daily changes in demand

→ protect against suppliers who may let you down.

Keeping little or no stock, which is necessary for many home-based businesses, has advantages and disadvantages. It tends to suit businesses in markets that are developing quickly, where products are expensive to buy and store in bulk, and where goods lose value or perish quickly. It means that you can be efficient and flexible – you only have stock when you need it, and you will have lower, if any, storage costs. You can also keep up to date with market trends and develop new products without wasting existing stock. On the other hand, you're dependent on the efficiency of your suppliers and may have to turn down orders if you can't meet immediate demand. Meeting stock needs at short notice can also become expensive.

By keeping lots of stock, you won't run the risk of running out and will be able to respond to sales quickly. Buying stock in bulk is also often cheaper, but that has to be weighed against the fact that you will possibly have higher storage and insurance costs, and the stock may date or become damaged before it's used. It also means that your capital is tied up in stock.

Keeping lots of stock will be necessary for businesses where volume of sales is difficult to predict, where it can be stored cheaply and where the items of stock are not likely to date or perish.

It's a good idea to set up a recording system so that you can monitor your current stock levels and set a trigger level for when to re-order – that is the level to which the stock needs to drop before you re-order supplies. Setting the right trigger level is important: too low, and you will run out of stock and be unable to deliver on your promises to customers; too high, and money will be tied up in stock when cash flow is tight.

Money trouble

Being able to deal with money troubles with a cool head is all about being able to spot problems early, and act immediately to stop them spiralling into anxieties that keep you awake at night.

Here are some pitfalls that good financial planning should help you to avoid:

→ taking on financial commitments before the business can pay for them – for example, premises or staff

→ spending too much on marketing in the hope that it will result in sales

→ having no money set aside for major expenses – for example, repairs or temporary staff

→ failing to complete or update a business plan or a cash flow forecast

→ having no financial procedures or financial record keeping

→ failing to agree payment terms with customers in writing, meaning that payment is disputed or delayed

→ having no money put aside for tax purposes

→ failing to have a pricing strategy

→ failing to shop around for competitive suppliers.

Sometimes things just don't go to plan. Despite all your efforts and budgeting, you may find that your business starts to struggle to repay its bills. Even businesses that are attracting lots of customers can face difficulties, so it's important to plan what you will do if this happens.

Financial problems don't necessarily mean that your business has to close. If you can persuade your bank or another investor that your business has a future, they may agree to lend you more money. Or you could release cash by removing unnecessary expenses or persuading your customers to pay more promptly. The key is understanding why your business might be experiencing difficulties before taking any decisions about how you can resolve the problem.

Common money mistakes

You'll be pleased to hear that there are some easy ways to avoid some of the more common money mistakes people make. The most important checklist to keep in mind is:

→ **Record it** – all money coming in and out of the business.

→ **Evidence it** – all receipts and invoices.

→ **Keep it** – hold on to all cash books, computer files and evidence for six years.

'Sometimes things just don't go to plan'

STOP	THINK	TIP
→ You're in the shopping centre and realise that you need stationery for the shop. It's on special offer so you nip in and pay for it out of your wallet.	→ This is a business expense and a transaction that you will want to record in your cash book and evidence to HMRC.	→ Always carry your business bank card or a second wallet where you store business receipts. Check this wallet at the end of each day and transfer receipts into your cash book.
→ You run a business from home and your electricity bill arrives. Without thinking, you pay the bill from your personal account.	→ A portion of your electricity bill will be a business expense that you will want to account for in your cash book and show to HMRC.	→ Keep records of your utility bills. Speak to HMRC for advice on tax relief you may be able to claim for domestic bills relating to running your business.
→ You're out and about on the road and receive a cash payment from a customer.	→ This is business income, which you will want to record in your cash book as proof of payment.	→ Always carry invoices and receipts so that you can provide your customer with proof of payment.
→ You're completing your annual tax return and get a shock when you realise you need money to pay tax on your income.	→ As an employee, you don't have to think about arranging tax payments. Your employer does all that for you. Being self-employed means that you will have to be thinking about tax throughout the year not just at year-end.	→ Build in a margin for tax in your pricing and make sure that the proportion you have built into your price gets transferred and saved in a separate bank account ready for your annual tax return.
→ You start taking drawings from your business in your first month of trading having had good initial sales.	→ Very few businesses make enough money in the first 3–6 months of trading to cover their costs, let alone support you with a salary.	→ Keep a cash flow and update the document every month. Only take drawings when the business is making money and you can predict stable income to come.

It's no secret that businesses need cash to survive, but how you achieve this is another matter. By getting to grips with the fundamentals of managing finance, cash flow, and bookkeeping, you will have put the right foundations in place, and be better able to anticipate and deal with any troubles ahead.

Talk the talk

Personal survival budget

The minimum amount of money you need to take from the business to cover your personal spending.

Sales ledger

A record of every invoice issued, payments received and amounts owed to your business by your customers.

Purchase ledger

A record of every invoice received, payments made and amounts owed by your business to your suppliers.

Fixed costs (or indirect costs, overheads)

Costs to your business that stay the same whether your sales go up or down e.g. rent, heating, insurance.

Variable costs (or direct costs, cost of sales)

Costs that rise and fall in line as a result of selling your product or service e.g. raw materials, components, cost of transportation.

Pro forma invoice

An invoice sent before goods have been supplied, which allows the buyer to raise a purchase order.

'Think about the space you need'

five

Where to work

Finding the right space for your new business is something that can take a lot of time and effort – and cash. It's worth asking yourself whether you need premises for your business. Buying or renting premises will eat into profits that you might otherwise be able to keep. Launching an online, mail order or mobile business, whether as a temporary or permanent measure could save you a significant amount of cash, which will help during the first few months of trading.

Think of the type of business you are, the space you need, and what you can realistically afford. If you want to run a café, you will need to rent or buy premises. But if you want to sell sandwiches, is an expensive high street lease the only option? If your business is trading online or mail order, you could consider starting up in your own home, saving yourself huge expense at a crucial time. Starting up a mobile business might also be an option. Why ask your customers to come to you when you can go out there and get them?

'Why ask your customers to come to you when you can go out there and get them?'

My story

Lorna Knapman, Love Food

I grew up on a farm in Dorset and have always loved food. Becoming a mum reignited that passion, and I had the idea of putting on a food festival geared towards adults and children, where farmers could trade fairly. I was waitressing in a bar above a venue that I thought would be ideal – safe and enclosed. I found out how much it would cost to hire and started making cold calls to sell pitches. I made calls on my mobile phone from wherever I was. With a mobile and the internet, you don't necessarily need an office or premises.

I have now done 15 events. I have a box room in my house set up as an office, and a lock-up for the signage, marquees and any other equipment. A farmer keeps the straw bales that I use for seating, in return for a free pitch. It captures people's imagination that the festival is suddenly there, and then disappears again. I have got a few new sites and done a pop-up event in an office headquarters with 1000 employees. We set up a mini festival in their cafeteria as part of their environment week.

I thought about having an office for meetings, but it's another overhead. If I have a meeting with someone, I either go to where they're based or the venue. There's no point in investing money in a swanky unit with the best office furniture and pictures on the wall. It's better to spend money on equipment and promotion, and getting a name for yourself. The premises can come later. That's the beauty of having the internet, which can be your online office. With social networking like Twitter and Facebook, you have easy, instantaneous, and free ways of reaching people. I wouldn't want to base myself in the same place in any event. I want to take Love Food on tour to as many people as possible.

Home sweet home

There are lots of advantages to running your business from home, one of the best being that it's cheap. Your utility bills (electricity, phone, heating) may increase a little but you will save a lot on rent. It also saves time that would otherwise be spent on looking for and arranging premises. And of course, you don't have to commute!

But there can also be some potential problems. A home address might not make a good impression on customers and suppliers, and regular meetings with clients would mean a lot of travel expense for you. Using your home limits opportunities to expand once your business gets going. Then there is the problem of separating your work life from your personal life. Being at home all day and in the evenings as well means that it could be difficult to escape work. Try to be disciplined and set times to take a break from work and surroundings.

There are a number of legal requirements that apply to running a business from home:

→ If running a business will significantly change the use of the building or have an impact on the surrounding area, you may need planning permission to make alterations.

→ The Valuation Office Agency may decide that part of your home is being used for business purposes and will adjust the rateable value of the property accordingly. This means that instead of just paying council tax, you will also pay business rates.

→ If your home is a rented property, your tenancy agreement will probably forbid you from using your home as a business premises. Negotiating a change in the agreement will take time and could mean your rent increases.

→ If you have a mortgage, you may be prevented from running a business from your home. You will need to check with your mortgage lender before you begin trading.

→ If your home is the property of a Housing Association, you will need to inform them of your business plans.

A virtual option

If you are worried about the lack of professional image working from home might present, a **virtual office** could be the answer. Companies offering this service can provide you with a range of options, including a dedicated business line that will be answered in your company name, screened, and forwarded to your number wherever you are, a company voice-mail to catch out-of-hours calls, and a prime business address where post can be delivered and signed for. You could work from home and clients will be none the wiser. There is also the possibility of hiring meeting rooms on a daily basis, if you need to meet clients or set up a video conference with clients further away.

Going online

Whether you are setting up an online business or an office-based business, you will need a website at some stage. Websites have become a must-have marketing tool for most businesses, and can help you to attract sales, enhance your brand and keep you in touch with your customers. Important rules are that the website is well branded, consistent with other sales and marketing materials, and easy for people to navigate.

What worked for me

Sarah Tremellen, Bravissimo

Our original concept was to sell bras in a wide range of bigger sizes, in lots of different styles. We realised that we wouldn't be able to open a high street shop at first, as the cost of the stock would have been huge. The internet had not yet kicked in, so we looked at mail order. The big advantage of mail order is that you can access a bigger pool of customers. A shop is for people who shop in that vicinity, whereas for mail order and web, the pool is worldwide. As a niche business, being able to talk to a geographically wider range of people worked for us.

After a while, the feedback from customers was that we needed to open a shop, where they could see the products, and be fitted. We were very nervous, given that with shops, leases tend to last quite a few years and you are responsible for paying the rent, even if the shop fails and you close it. But our business is a destination business. Generally people shop with us because they know us and are planning to visit us, not because they have just walked past and thought they might fancy a big bra. So we can be off the high street, round the corner, and pay a third of the rent of a high street store. A business that relies on passing trade, e.g. a mainstream fashion retailer, would need the high street presence.

We started online sales in 1999, just as the internet was becoming mainstream. It sat very comfortably with mail order, as the back end – the order processing and packaging – is the same. Quickly it appeared that we'd get orders from people who had seen the magazine but ordered online. The magazine is still a big driver of our web traffic, so it has to be easy for customers to get the information from one to the other. The website has to be easy to use and represent what we are about. People can come and go in seconds, so if they don't get what it is about quite quickly, they won't stay. It has to be easy for people to buy things from the website. It may be a flashy design, but if you can't work out how to order your size or look at what is in the basket, that's going to frustrate customers and hinder sales.

Web design is a specialised area, and I would recommend seeking expert advice on how to do it, in order to get the most out of the branding, the structure, and mechanics such as search engine optimisation.

Most importantly, our shops, mail order magazine, and our website must work together. They must all look like they come from the same place.

Hard earned money is wasted designing a professional website if your customers can't find you online. Make the most of every opportunity to list and direct interest to your website:

➜ List your website address on all your promotional materials including adverts, letterheads, leaflets, business cards, calling cards and packaging.

➜ Find a domain name (and register it) that is the same or similar to your business name so that customers stand a better chance of guessing right in a search engine.

➜ Make sure you optimise your website – that your web pages are ranked highly by search engines.

'Websites are a must-have marketing tool'

Get those hits

People have become used to looking for things online via search engines, and there are steps that can be taken that could mean your website appears higher in search companies' website rankings. That means that when a potential customer puts your business name, or their best guess, into a search engine, your website will appear high up on the list of relevant websites – making it easy for your customers to find you. This process of making small modifications to your website to improve its search engine ranking is called search engine optimisation (SEO). This is a very technical area and it would be a good idea to use a specialist web designer to increase SEO. There are however, some steps you can take to increase visibility.

The title of your homepage should include your business name and website address and could also include other important information like your location and your mission statement.

Make sure that all the web pages that make up your website have titles and aren't 'Untitled' or tell the user nothing about the content, for example, 'Page 1'. If you list short titles that relate to the content of each page, it's more likely that the search engine will list the page title in a search result.

You can add general interest pages to your website so that other websites will link to your website. Search engines use the number of but, most importantly, the quality of the inbound links as an indicator of the quality of your website. You might want to list news articles, press releases, reports and statistics to attract well respected websites to link to your website. But think carefully about the sites that you choose to link to; you are directing traffic away from your website and creating associations with the content listed on other websites.

I need premises – but where and what?

If you decide to take up business premises, think what you will need it to do for you. If you'll only use it for storage, you won't need much more than space and security, but if customers or suppliers will be visiting, your premises will need to create the right impression.

Before you make any decisions, think about:

→ **Location, location, location** – is your business likely to rely partly on 'passing trade'? If so, it would be better for you to be located somewhere customers are likely to be passing rather than on an industrial estate. Check out what the surrounding area is like at different times of day. Do you need to have good transport links for example, if you're importing/exporting goods or shipping goods across the UK, or if you and your staff will need to travel frequently?

→ **Your customers** – if you're planning to run a shop or office open to the public, you'll need somewhere convenient for customers and deliveries.

→ **Your staff** – can your staff get there easily and will they need parking?

→ **Your competitors** – sometimes, pitching your business just up the road from a competitor can be a good thing; estate agents and coffee shops tend to be close neighbours as well as competitors. This can help you keep tabs on your competitors' next moves. An area can also become well known for the quality or value of its restaurants or shops, and sourcing premises in this area would place your business in a particular area of the market.

Top tip

When searching for business premises, talk to the local council about whether there are any planned changes to the area that could have a damaging effect on your business. For example, major road works scheduled for your street.

➔ **How much space you need** – the more space you have, the more it will cost but don't feel that you have to cramp yourself either. Consider how much stock you will need to store on the business premises. Will you need space for meetings? It is also useful to draw a plan of how you want the furniture and equipment arranged, then try to estimate how much space it will all take – in square feet or metres.

➔ **Access** – it's important that your product or service will be accessible to disabled people. The Disability Discrimination Act requires that you take reasonable steps to accommodate disabled people, which may mean fitting handrails, widening doorways and adding access ramps to a property. You may want to consider these requirements, certainly when sourcing property, but also when building a website for your business. You may, for example, need to enable large print or audio functions on the site.

> **Top tip**
>
> Before you make any significant changes to your premises, check whether you will need planning permission.

➔ **Secure storage space** – consider whether the location you have in mind is safe for your type of business. If, for example, you're a painter, decorator, joiner, fitter or gardener you will need space to lock up your equipment – a small warehouse or a garage would be ideal.

➔ **Cost** – calculate whether you can afford the rent. There is likely to be significant cost to your business up front to secure the property – for example, an advance on the rent. Can you also afford the business rates, water rates, utility costs and any maintenance or management fees?

➔ **Health and safety** – you have a legal responsibility to make sure that your business premises are safe for you, any employees and your customers.

➔ **Restrictions** – there may be restrictions on where you can run your business – for example, on the amount of noise you will make or the materials you use to make your product.

Renting ...

Renting is a good option if you want to have a proper business address but can't afford to buy. However, make sure it's the best option for you before signing a lease – it can be really difficult, if not impossible, to get out of a lease at a later date. A lease gives you certain obligations, so seek legal advice before making a commitment.

The terms of your lease depend on what you negotiate with the landlord. A typical lease normally requires that you occupy the property for an agreed **term** and pay an agreed monthly rent. The lease may allow the rent to be reviewed periodically. You are normally required to pay small amounts up front to secure the lease such as an advance on the first month's rent. You may also have to pay a premium to purchase the lease and professional fees, for example, if you are liaising with an estate agent.

Renting will generally allow you more flexibility, but it's important that you negotiate the terms of a lease with a clear picture of your business needs, both now and some years into the future. If you expect your business to grow, leasing might be the best option. As you require more space you can move into a larger building without the hassle of having to sell original premises.

Top tip

Check out a revised code of practice that can be helpful in negotiating favourable rates on **commercial leases.** It contains tips on understanding terms and conditions of leases.

My story

Justin Douglas, Fall Off the Wall

When we first set up our creative design agency, we worked from a bedroom at home to keep costs down. With minimal overheads, we undercut anyone we could to get the business, using contacts we had built up from old companies.

Six months later we moved into the Hat Factory, an arts facility in the centre of Luton that aims to develop the arts in the town and surrounding region. The Hat Factory served its purpose, as it was a government funded incubation centre for young businesses. As well as being pretty cheap, it gave us the chance to network with other people and build relationships, particularly people who could help us with some of the work for the clients we had.

As we grew, it became clear that we would need more space. We only had one office, and we needed to separate the sales and creative environment. We wanted creatives in their own space where they could think and be creative rather than sitting in a busy, noisy sales office.

We've now moved out to the countryside, to offices in the heart of a forest. We have four times the space and it's a great place for clients to come. You can portray yourself in a positive light, full of positive energy in a natural environment. Clients want to buy into that and to you as a company.

Any landlord will be looking to rent to somebody reliable and low-risk to whom they can pass on most of the costs of the lease. Here are some things to think about when you're budgeting to rent a business property:

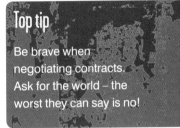

Top tip

Be brave when negotiating contracts. Ask for the world – the worst they can say is no!

→ **Legal and search fees** – in addition to solicitors' fees, you may incur local authority and environmental costs when searching for a property.

→ **Deposit/guarantee** – you'll need to pay the landlord a deposit before your business can move in.

→ **Rent and service costs** – payments are usually made every three months and some payment will be required in advance to secure the property.

→ **VAT** – value added tax will be payable on rent and **service charges**.

→ **Stamp duty and land tax** – these fees are normally payable on granting the lease.

→ **Land registry fees** – depending on the length of your lease you may have to pay a fee to have the lease registered.

→ **Repairs** – your lease may require you to take care of repairs or general maintenance.

→ **Utilities** – will you need to pay for electricity or lighting? Utilities are sometimes shared between other business tenants so ask for a rough estimate. Landlords must provide prospective tenants with an energy performance certificate, which indicates how energy efficient a building and its services are, and can act as a good indicator of likely energy costs. You may be able to cut down the bills by, for example, ensuring the air conditioning systems and boilers are well maintained.

→ **Phone and internet** – how much will you need to pay for line rental and call charges?

→ **Insurance** – is the building insured already? Will you need to secure it against theft or vandalism?

PROS

• Most commercial properties are already set up for businesses with telephone lines, suitable lighting and security arrangements.

• Renting premises will give your business the status of a proper address, which can be added to letters and business cards.

CONS

• A lease binds you to a particular property and regular rental payments for a set amount of time. You may be able to transfer it to another business if you decide to move, but there's no guarantee you'll find another business willing to take it on.

• Getting consent from the owner to make alterations may be difficult.

• You may take on significant repair or maintenance obligations, which can be costly.

• Your rental payments may increase over the period of your lease in line with market trends.

... Or buying?

Making a decision about buying a commercial property is not one to be taken lightly. Your property could be your biggest and most expensive asset, so it's important to make a well-informed decision. There are lots of advantages to owning commercial property but it's important to look at the needs of your business to help you to decide whether buying is the best option for you.

Unless you are able to access a large amount of capital to purchase a property in cash you will need to take out a commercial mortgage on business premises. Most banks and building societies offer commercial mortgages but each lender will offer different rates so it's important to shop around, or even use a commercial mortgage broker who can compare the deals for you. A lender will need to be satisfied that you meet specific criteria in order to take out a commercial mortgage, such as a positive credit rating and evidence that your business is creditworthy. Bear in mind that you will typically be committing to a minimum mortgage term of 15 years and will have to provide details of your business accounts and cash flow to the lender.

PROS

- Buying a property means that you will own a large asset that may increase in value.
- You may be able to find and afford a building with more space than you need, allowing you to sublet or expand at a later date.
- You can remortgage to raise finance for your business.
- You can design or alter the premises to suit the needs of your business.

CONS

- You need to raise a large deposit in order to secure the purchase of a property.
- Owning premises will make it harder to relocate if you decide to expand.
- Owning a property means that you will be responsible for any maintenance and repair costs, which can be unpredictable and expensive.

Making the move

Before moving into your new building, it's important to take a look at your budget and to put aside money to pay for:

→ removal costs from your current property (if you have one) – van hire, professional cleaning fees

→ decorating costs – repainting your new property, recarpeting

→ furnishings – buying office furniture and equipment

→ communications – setting up computer networks, broadband connection, and telephone systems

→ stationery – designing and ordering branded stationery.

Talk the talk

Virtual office

An office that does not have one physical location but can be set up by you anywhere, using a combination of address and technology services.

Commercial lease/business tenancy

A legal agreement between you (the tenant) and the owner of the premises you will be renting (the landlord).

Duration/term

The length of time an agreement lasts. A lease agreement may last for between six months and several years.

Service charge

Extra charges (which may be included in the rental payments) for things like window cleaning.

'The law protects you and your, customers'

six

The legal bit

There are many laws and regulations that can affect your business. Some are designed to protect you. Others protect your customers, the public or your employees. Some laws and regulations apply to all businesses whereas others only affect businesses of certain types, or those operating in specific sectors. This chapter will highlight some of the more common legal requirements but the only way to ensure you run your business within the law is to thoroughly research the rules that apply.

Licences

Some businesses need to apply for licences before they start trading. The rules are different depending on the type of business, for example:

→ Food businesses need a licence from the environmental health department.

→ Businesses selling alcohol need two different licences.

→ Businesses dealing with children need a special licence that is renewed annually.

Your local authority will be able to tell you whether any licences are needed for your business. For further information on where to find help, turn to the directory at the back of the book.

'You'll need insurance as soon as you start trading'

Business insurance

All businesses need insurance as soon as they start trading. Some types of insurance are required by law and should be in place before you are up and running. For example, you must have motor insurance if you drive a car or you must have employers' **liability** insurance if you employ people. Other types are optional but worth considering, as uninsured losses could put you out of business or leave you in debt. For example, if you borrowed money to buy tools for your business and those tools were stolen, you would still have to repay the money you borrowed even though you wouldn't have the tools to operate your business. Insurance could have covered the cost of replacing the tools.

You're likely to need a combination of insurance **policies** that might include:

→ Motor insurance: if you own and use a car, then you must have at least third party motor insurance. The policy will protect you against claims for any injury or damage sustained in a car accident involving your vehicle. If your car is currently issued for personal use, you must tell your insurer if you intend to start using it for your business. If you use your car to transport business goods, you will need to buy a separate policy to cover 'goods in transit' which is discussed below.

→ Property insurance: for your business assets such as machinery, plant, tools, buildings, stock and other equipment, including 'goods in transit'. All risks cover is best, as it means you will be covered for any accidental loss or damage – for example by fire, severe weather or theft – to the property that you have insured, apart from those items listed as exclusions. Most property insurance policies will include an 'excess'. If your policy states that you have an excess of £100 then you will not be covered for the first £100 of any claim that you make. If you put in a claim for £500 and the insurance company accepts it, you would receive £400. The amount of the excess will vary between insurers. Whether or not you need to insure the property itself will depend on whether you own it. If you lease the premises, check with your landlord.

→ Employers' liability insurance: is compulsory if you employ anyone, even part time or temporarily. The policy will protect you against any claims that might be made against you if they are killed, injured or become ill as a result of the work they do for you.

→ Public liability insurance: covers you in case someone sues you for injury or damage you cause them or their property.

→ Product liability insurance: protects you against claims for injury or damage caused by the products you make.

You could try and buy insurance direct or on the internet, but it can be very time-consuming, and your time is probably better spent on running the business. An insurance broker will be able to explain exactly which types of insurance your business needs, and be able to find you a competitive price.

> **Top tip**
>
> Make sure that you have all the relevant insurance policies in place at the right time. For example, you might need buildings and contents cover before you officially start to trade. When drawing up your budget, remember to include the costs of any licences and insurance policies you need.

Health and safety

As a business owner, you are responsible for the health and safety of your employees, customers and anyone else who may be affected by your business, for example visitors to your premises or anyone affected by the products/services you design, produce and supply. The principles of health and safety are about protecting people from harm and illness by taking precautions and providing a safe working environment. Different types of business have different requirements and considerations.

The Health & Safety Executive (HSE) and your local authority make sure that the law on various aspects of health and safety is being followed. They are a good source of information when you need help and advice on health and safety issues. The HSE website has a wide range of information, guides, leaflets and forms on various aspects of health and safety law.

Some of the health and safety issues that you will need to consider are listed overleaf. This doesn't cover everything but is a good starting point.

'Health and safety is about protecting people from harm'

Risk assessments and policies

You should carry out a thorough assessment of the risks your business faces. You also need to have a policy for how you look after health and safety. If you employ five or more people, the policy must be in writing. You will need to tell staff about fire risks, put emergency arrangements in place, and provide training in fire safety procedures and escape drills.

Legal requirements that you will need to comply with include:

→ recording and reporting accidents

→ consulting employees or their safety representatives on health and safety matters

→ making sure your employees understand and carry out their responsibilities for health and safety, for example following the safety rules you have set up.

Special regulations also exist for certain types of businesses that do one or more of the following things:

→ work in a factory or workshop

→ use heavy machinery

→ use hazardous substances (like chemicals or pesticides)

→ do a lot of lifting and carrying

→ work in dusty or dangerous environments – for example, in very high or very low temperatures.

Although registration with your local authority or with the Health & Safety Executive (HSE) is no longer necessary, you may still have to register under other regulations, depending on your type of business. If you don't know whether you need to register, contact your local HSE or local authority office to check.

You need to protect employees and others who could be at risk from the use of dangerous substances in your business. You must also comply with the smoking ban in public places, workplaces and company vehicles used by more than one person, which is enforced by local authorities.

There are also activity risks in many types of workplace, for example:

➜ using many types of machinery and equipment

➜ driving

➜ poorly designed workstations, or working without a break, which can harm computer and other display screen equipment users

➜ back injuries caused by poor lifting and carrying practices, activities that create excessive noise, and falls, still the biggest killer on construction sites.

You must include the well-known risks in your particular industry in the risk assessment. You must also take into account the capabilities, training, knowledge and experience of your workers. Make sure that the demands of the job don't exceed their ability to carry out their work without risk to themselves and others.

Occupational health

You need to take responsibility for the general welfare of your employees. You are legally required to meet various basic standards, like providing adequate space, lighting and toilet facilities. Generally, you should ensure your employees enjoy a healthy working environment and good working practices.

My story

Nigel Tait, N Tait Services

I had worked for an electrical contracting firm, but was signed off sick, and didn't work for five years. When I decided to start my own business, I wanted it to be as stress-free and hassle-free as possible. My accountant suggested I set up as a sole trader. He said that a limited company would mean more bookwork and cost more with accountancy fees.

I started up on my own two and a half years ago, and now have a dozen residential letting agents on my books and do 3–4 jobs a day, mainly fixing domestic electrical appliances.

There has been quite a bit of paperwork, but it hasn't been scary. It's not my favourite thing and my mentor is always nagging me to keep it up to date, but it is very important.

You have to make sure you are registered with income tax people and also check out the relevant legislation. I knew about health and safety from my work before. For electrical work I have to have Part P registration so that I can do work in domestic dwellings. The electrical regulations changed just as I was starting up, so I had to go on a course. I heard about that through word of mouth, so it's good to keep your eyes and ears open. But now I am registered, they keep me up to date. I need public liability cover. It wasn't hard to find out about it. You can ring governing bodies, the tax office, your local council on building regulations – they are all there to help. Having a mentor who has been in business for a number of years himself has also been a tremendous help. I would just say don't be scared and always ask for help.

Data protection

It doesn't matter how small your business is, the Data Protection Act 1998 will affect you if you are storing information about customers, suppliers or employees. It also doesn't matter how that information is stored, whether in a filing cabinet or on a computer. If you break the law, you could face a fine and court costs.

The point of the Act is to protect the way in which personal information is used. Provided certain principles are followed, businesses can use personal information if the person concerned has agreed, or if there is a valid reason for using that information. There are stricter rules for 'sensitive information' – on health, religious beliefs or previous convictions, for example.

According to the law:

→ Information you keep must be stored securely and responsibly. This means you must use passwords on computers and keep filing cabinets locked. It's a good idea to keep visitors away from the most sensitive areas of your office so data cannot be seen accidentally – by an IT contractor, perhaps.

→ You must explain what the information will be used for. For example, if you're making a list of your customers so that you can send them mailshots, you must first ask if they're happy for you to do this, and for you to continue sending mailshots of similar products or services your business provides.

→ You can only keep information for a specified reason.

→ You can't keep information for longer than is necessary.

→ You can't share the information without permission.

→ You must tell people that you are storing the information and people can request access to the information you hold about them. If they ask, you must provide it within 40 days, although you can charge them a fee of up to £10.

Personal information on the monitoring of workers, including casual, contract and agency staff – which could include the monitoring of e-mails – is also covered by the Act. In order to help businesses stay on the right side of the law, The Information Commissioner's Office has developed a code of best practice. The code states that workers should be made aware of why and how they are being monitored, and that if the monitoring has any adverse effects, there must be good reason for this.

Top tip

Get professional legal advice before making any major business decisions. Even if you think you know what you can and cannot do, the law can change.

Some businesses have to register with the Information Commissioner, depending on why they are storing information. If the personal information you are processing is for staff administration – things like payroll, advertising, and marketing for your own business, accounts and records, then generally you will not need to register.

Intellectual property

Intellectual property refers to things a business creates that can be protected by law. These can be things like inventions, music, drawings, photographs, books, articles and computer programs. Your intellectual property rights can be some of the most valuable assets that your business owns. They can set you apart from your competitors, offer customers something new and different and be sold or licensed, providing a good source of income.

The four main types of intellectual property are:

→ **patents** for inventions, new and improved products that can be used in some kind of industry

→ **trademarks** for signs, logos, words used to protect brand identity – like the McDonald's Golden Arches or the Coca-Cola glass bottle

→ designs for the appearance of whole or part of a product

→ **copyright** for original text, images, music, film, sound recordings and broadcasts, software and multimedia.

The law explains the rights of intellectual property owners and helps them protect their rights. Some intellectual property rights apply automatically, like copyright, for example. You automatically own the copyright in any literary, dramatic, musical or artistic works (including information booklets and computer programs) that you or your employees create, and 'fix' in written or recorded form. People cannot use or copy your work without permission (for which you could charge a fee). Protection extends to use on the internet and in most cases, will last until 70 years after the death of the creator.

Other intellectual property rights, such as patents and trademarks, have to be registered at the Intellectual Property Office (IPO). Patent registration can be a time-consuming and expensive process. It takes up to three years to get a patent in the UK, and longer in Europe and the US. It will last up to twenty years from the day you register it, although after four years must be renewed every year. Registering a trademark is more straightforward – it will cost a few hundred pounds and must be renewed every ten years. It's worth bearing in mind that registering your company name at Companies House does not mean that it has a trademark.

Understanding the law surrounding intellectual property will mean that you can make the best use out of your own. You will know how to protect it, sell it, and license it. Understanding its importance will also help you not to use other people's intellectual property without permission – whether it's using copies of software without a licence or taking a photo and accidentally including someone else's artwork in the background.

'Your intellectual property rights can be some of your most valuable assets'

What worked for me

Nick Jenkins, Moonpig.com

As an internet business, our domain name is one of our biggest assets. It is the door to our shop, so it was important to have it registered to us directly and be able to control any changes to it.

The Moonpig brand is also very important to us and we trademarked our name to prevent anyone else from using it. I used a trademark lawyer, which made it quite straight-forward and it cost about £1000. It seemed quite a lot of money when we were starting out, but now if you look at where we are, it was a very important thing to get right.

We didn't apply for patents on the software we wrote covering the process of personalising cards online. Our protection was that we got on and did it better and quicker than anyone else. You can get so wound up spending time and money trying to protect an idea, and not actually develop it commercially. It's the kind of thing they always ask on Dragons' Den, and it may be useful for genuine inventions, but in reality it costs a lot and takes time. You have to ask how protectable is your idea? How easy is it to define what you have done? Could someone find another way around it? And do you have the money and legal firepower to defend it if someone does copy it?

When you're starting out, you shouldn't spend much money on legal advice before researching what is available for free on Government funded websites. You also need to understand the core legal issues yourself. It is no use assuming that your lawyer will think of everything for you. Some things might seem irrelevant when you are small, but if you are successful, things can come back to haunt you – as that's when there are things worth fighting over! If you are trying to raise investment, it's critical that you understand the purpose of the articles of association and shareholders agreement. New investors will normally ask for a new shareholders' agreement that gives them certain rights to control key decisions. If you are not careful you can lose control of your own firm.

On a smaller scale, if you're starting out with a friend, try to think ahead a few steps. What if one of you dies or you disagree on an issue? How will these things be resolved? If you agree these things in writing upfront, it saves the heartache of trying to sort it out later. The problem with verbal agreements is that people forget what they said at the time.

Employment law

If your business employs people, you have to comply with a number of legal requirements. These are in place to protect the rights of the people who work for you. Employment law covers:

→ working hours and holidays

→ pensions

→ **discrimination**

→ wages and conditions

→ tax and National Insurance

→ employment contracts

→ job descriptions

→ maternity and parental leave

→ employers' liability insurance.

It's best to get professional advice in order to avoid running into problems with your staff. For further information on where to find help, turn to the directory at the back of the book.

'Treating employees equally and fairly has the knock-on effect of improving performance'

Policies

Although work **policies** are voluntary, they can help make sure that you stay within the law, and are consistent with all employees. If employees believe they are being treated equally and fairly, this can have the knock-on effect of improving performance. Some policies, covering environmental issues and equal opportunities, for example, can also help positively raise your profile with potential customers. Some of the areas that you might want to consider having a policy for include:

→ working practices – including hours, time off, pay and rewards

→ equality and diversity

→ redundancy

→ intellectual property and confidential information

→ smoking, drugs and alcohol

→ e-mail, internet and phone use

→ environment – not only can this help save costs by reducing waste, energy, and use of supplies; it could improve your business reputation, which could be vital if dealing with larger organisations.

Some policies also come with legal requirements:

→ health and safety – you must have a policy to cover health and safety if you have five or more employees

→ discipline and grievance procedures – you must set out your disciplinary rules, and disciplinary and grievance procedures, in writing.

You must tell each employee about:

➔ your disciplinary rules and procedure

➔ your dismissal and grievance procedure

➔ the name of the person employees must contact if they are unhappy about a disciplinary or dismissal decision, or to put right a complaint.

You can include information on policies in the employee's written statement, or alternatively the written statement can tell the employee where they can read it, for example in a staff handbook.

Online information

If your business is a limited company or limited liability partnership, (LLP), the information that you normally display on business stationery has to be displayed on websites and e-mails. This includes your full company name, registration number and registered office address, e-mail address and VAT number. You also need to explain to website visitors and customers the terms and conditions of use, including standard contractual information if you are conducting business online. You don't need to put the company information and terms and conditions on every page. Putting it in an 'about us' page will do. However, if you don't include it anywhere, you could end up being fined. If you are a sole trader and you use a trading name, you must include your own name and business address on your website (and on business documents).

Consumer protection

Understanding your customers' rights will not only help if a dispute arises, it can help build your business reputation and retain customers. On average, an unhappy customer tells 10 people about their experience, who will each talk to other people about it. Understanding what your customer can expect of you will help avoid this scenario.

If you have sold or hired goods to a customer, that customer has the following rights:

→ the goods must match the description you give of them

→ they must be of satisfactory quality

→ they must be fit for the purpose.

The customer has these rights against the supplier of the goods, i.e. you, if you have sold them, rather than the manufacturer. If these rights have not been met, the consumer can reject the goods (within six years), which would mean you having to pay a refund and compensation where necessary.

If you provide a service to a customer, the work has to be carried out by you with reasonable skill and care, and you must also provide the service within a 'reasonable' amount of time and at a 'reasonable' price, if, in your contract with the customer, you haven't set out exact dates and prices.

If the service you have provided is unsatisfactory and you haven't used reasonable skill, you will have to put the work right without charging extra. Otherwise, the customer can ask another supplier to put things right and then claim the other supplier's costs back from you.

Talk the talk

Liability

Being legally responsible for any problems that occur as a result of your business's activity.

Policies

The principles that guide the decisions to be taken in a certain area. There is no legal requirement to follow a policy, just guidance as to what ought to be done.

Discrimination

Behaviour towards a certain group, for example women, that involves excluding or restricting members of that group from opportunities that are available to other groups.

Trademarks

Symbols that distinguish goods and services in the marketplace – like logos and brand names.

Patents

Protection on the features and processes that make things work, that allows inventors to make money from their inventions.

Copyright

An automatic right that protects work once it is fixed, that is written or recorded in some way.

'How you speak
is just as
important as
what you say'

seven

Selling yourself

There are many different parts to setting up and running a successful business. There is your idea, your product or service, your finances – and you. How you behave makes a huge difference to your business, your employees and your customers. Everyone you come into contact with – customers, suppliers, even your bank manager – will form impressions and make decisions based on how you present yourself. The more professional you are in your dealings with people, the more faith people will have in your business.

Get the message across

Being able to communicate effectively with staff, partners and the general public is essential if you are going to run a successful business. Don't worry if this is not something that comes naturally. Good communication skills can be learned, but it's important to practise regularly in order to be confident in any situation, whether it's a business meeting, sales presentation or social engagement with a client.

'Good communication skills can be learned'

The language barrier

The way that you speak to people and the type of language you use can have a major impact on whether people take your ideas and business proposals seriously. People make a judgement of you within the first few seconds of meeting you and *how* you speak is just as important as *what* you say. A person will instinctively form an impression based on your tone of voice, your accent and the language you choose to use.

Here are some tips to keep in mind to make sure you communicate effectively:

→ Speak clearly, in a calm and polite manner.

→ Focus on the positive. Always give and receive positives rather than negatives because it keeps the conversation upbeat.

→ Mirror the other person. If their comments are short and succinct, make sure yours are too. This helps to create a relaxed and positive atmosphere where all feel equal.

→ If you are talking to one other person, make and hold eye contact with them – but don't stare them out!

→ In groups, speak to the whole group. Bring your eyes to rest on different people in the group and respond to any questions by including everyone.

→ Get your point across quickly. Think about the key things you want to say before you say them to make sure that you don't ramble.

Top tip

Here are some tricks to play on yourself if you're feeling nervous:

→ Have a business alter ego to help you get through nerve-racking situations – for example, picture yourself as a world leader giving a powerful speech.

→ Focus on your tone of voice and your breathing and relax your shoulders as you speak.

→ Wear clothes and shoes you feel comfortable in.

→ Know when to take the meeting 'offline': i.e. when to continue the discussion privately or on another occasion if, say, too much detail is being discussed.

→ Avoid slang, jargon and swearing that may cause offence.

→ Avoid unhelpful clichés, like 'Failure is not an option.'

→ Try not to fidget with your hair or clothes – it will distract from what you're saying.

→ Be aware of your body. People make judgments based on your body language. You can be supportive when you're not speaking by nodding your head slowly, making eye contact, facing the speaker and making other gestures that show you're interested.

My story

David Scott, Phoenix Roofing

I worked for a national roofing company when I left school, but they weren't offering good service and I didn't want to be part of it. We were being asked to do things we weren't trained to do, and they ended up on Watchdog.

I did some leadwork training, and set up my own company doing leadwork for churches and older buildings, and then got into green roofs too. I've since gone into partnership with an established pitch roof company.

Teamwork is vital within our company and with other companies. We try and assist each other where we can, as what goes around comes around. Nine times out of ten you will get a favour back.

I think with suppliers, and even with clients, it is good to be firm, but without being rude. In this market, people try and take what they can, and are constantly trying to get us to do a little bit extra. If you say yes, it gives them the scope to push you around and to not treat you professionally. If you are straight with them, they accept it and have a little bit more respect for you. We still get repeat work from them.

It is a big transition from being 'on the tools' to where I am now, office-based. A lot of guys who do it think and act like they're still on site. They talk the same way to clients, prospective clients and staff, and a lot of it is lost in translation. Clients and people like quantity surveyors or office managers are different to a foreman. You have to adapt and be flexible. It's the more common touch with people outside, the lads and manual workers on site. You can say it how it is. But you have to be more careful and more articulate with office people. It's all in the way you deliver what you are saying.

Giving presentations

Sometimes you will need to give a presentation to a group of people, whether to potential clients at a competitive pitch, the bank, a Business Angel to attract investment or an event at which you can promote your business. It can be nerve-wracking to face a room full of people, many of whom will have sat through many presentations before and will be looking to hear something that stands out. Here are some tips to help make your words the most memorable thing they hear that day:

→ Prepare your presentation in advance.

→ Know your audience – ask about the venue, who and how many will be attending, understand the purpose of the presentation, and keep these details in mind when preparing.

→ Structure your presentation with a clear beginning, middle and end.

→ Present an agenda or the topic headings – it will help your audience to spot where you are in the presentation.

→ Practise your presentation in the mirror – it will help you to adjust your body language and movement.

→ Make sure your gestures and body language match the size of your audience – the bigger the audience, the bolder your gestures.

→ Scan the audience to give people the impression you're addressing them individually.

→ For big venues, pick a spot at the back of the audience and project your voice to the last few rows in the audience.

→ Don't read your speech word for word – use prompt cards.

→ Don't rush your speech – pause after each sentence to allow you to breathe and your audience to understand what you've just said.

→ Use key messages – if you are in a pitch, give people three reasons why you should get the business. Get across key points about your business in the first three minutes – for example, the cost of your product or service, where it will sell, how it will sell, who it will sell to and the profit it will make.

→ Anticipate questions and prepare answers – you'll impress if you have the answers up your sleeve ready.

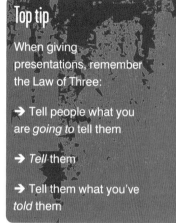

Top tip

When giving presentations, remember the Law of Three:

→ Tell people what you are *going to* tell them

→ *Tell* them

→ Tell them what you've *told* them

The write words?

Effective writing can help you build relationships, save time and run your business efficiently. It goes without saying that bad writing can undo all of this good work.

Here are some tips to help you write effective e-mails and letters:

→ Use a standard business format for your letters and be consistent – for example, if you begin a letter with 'Dear Joe Bloggs', end the letter with 'Yours sincerely' and if you don't know the person's name, begin with 'Dear Sir/Madam' and end with 'Yours faithfully'.

→ An e-mail is more informal but it's still important to be professional. Always end an e-mail with 'Best regards' or 'Kind regards'.

→ Always give the purpose of your letter or e-mail in the opening sentence. You could start with 'I am writing with regard to…'

→ Don't spend fifteen words expressing something you could put in five – less is more!

→ Check for spelling errors. Don't rely on your computer's spell-check function but proof-read yourself.

→ Ask a friend, colleague or mentor to proof-read materials for you – particularly marketing materials that will cost a lot of money to correct after they've been printed.

→ Keep a copy of important letters and e-mails you send for future reference.

E-tiquette

Here are some golden rules to keep in mind when writing and sending e-mails:

→ Never, ever write and send an e-mail when you're feeling angry, upset or under pressure – remember that once an e-mail is sent, what you have written remains on record, and could be forwarded and read by somebody else. Ask yourself whether you would be happy with that, and if the answer is 'no', play safe and don't send it.

→ Avoid sending e-mail forwards or jokes.

→ People send and receive hundreds of e-mails every day – ask yourself whether every man and his dog needs to receive your e-mail and only send to the most appropriate people.

→ If you're sending a lot of information by e-mail, an attached report can be more effective than simply a long e-mail; be careful that attachments aren't too big!

→ Protect people's privacy – if you're sending an e-mail to a mailing list, know how to use the blind copy function.

Acting professional

When you've arranged to meet someone, whether it's a customer, supplier or an investor, it's important to present yourself in a professional manner. People will make judgements on you based on how you look and present yourself. Adopting a professional manner can help you to feel more confident and business-like.

Here are some things to remember when meeting someone:

→ **Punctuality** – be on time, or even a few minutes early.

→ **Personal presentation** – dress smartly and make sure you look clean and tidy.

→ **Professional behaviour** – shake hands, wait to be offered a seat, make eye contact and be polite. Thank the person for their time.

→ **Sell yourself** – be confident, enthusiastic and well-prepared.

→ **Follow-up** – make notes about what was discussed and make sure you stick to any deadlines agreed.

→ **Feedback** – ask for feedback after the meeting, and be prepared to change things that didn't work.

What works for me

Geoff Quinn, T.M.Lewin

I have the same core values at work and home, but I just go about things differently. At work I make decisions quickly and push things through. At home I take my foot off the accelerator. I have an hour train journey every day and I can feel myself changing. At home, my wife takes charge and we probably wouldn't have a holiday if she wasn't there. If I was like that at work, we probably wouldn't have a business.

Life is like play acting. You can understand your role, whether it's a meeting or a network event and morph into it. But you have to be sincere: if you are trying to be something that you are not, you will have problems.

If, when you meet people, you want to leave a positive impression at the end, you have to give the right first impression at the beginning. And that is about preparation. Think about what are you hoping to achieve with that person and the impression you want them to have of you. Every day before I get dressed, I see what meetings I have and then dress appropriately.

Like most people, I am quick to form a first impression. I hate people being late or unprepared for a meeting. When they arrive, I look at what people are wearing, and then whether they look like a frightened rabbit or they are confident. How strong is their handshake? Do they have good eye contact? Some people take time to warm up, but you have already formed an impression of them and you are waiting for them to confirm that impression.

I used to watch Chris, the guy that bought T.M.Lewin, and the way that he talked to people, greeted them, and his mannerisms. In the end I sounded like him. I would watch the way he did the job and followed through and I would copy the bits I liked. I was always that wide-eyed person that took in everything. I listened to the way people talked, the nuances, so that if I was in that situation I could sound older than I was. I still pick up tips today when looking around.

Hosting meetings

→ Before organising a meeting, make sure you are confident that a meeting is needed and that it has a clear purpose – for example, to come up with a solution to a problem or to prepare for a sales meeting.

Top tip

Before the meeting, make sure that all attendees agree with the agenda – and if not, make sure a compromise is reached so that you can make progress at the meeting.

→ Decide who needs to be at the meeting – make sure that the people you invite are knowledgeable and/or senior enough to make decisions.

→ Send out an agenda – the list of topics that you will discuss – in advance. That way everyone can come to the meeting prepared.

→ Decide in advance how you will run the meeting, and what tools, like flipchart materials and pens, you will need.

→ It's professional to have a quiet and private space in which to host your meeting, so try to book a room in advance.

→ Always take spare copies of any paperwork along for anyone who may have forgotten theirs.

→ Give an introduction to the meeting – ask people to introduce themselves and tell others a bit about their role. Tell people the purpose of the meeting and what you want to achieve.

→ Know when to ask open and closed questions – for example, you should use **open questions** when you want discussion and **closed questions** when you want to agree a decision or bring discussion to an end.

➜ Be clear about what you decide during the meeting – repeat each decision as it's made, who will be responsible for acting on a decision and record each decision clearly in the **minutes**.

➜ Have tea and coffee available – biscuits usually go down well too!

➜ Always finish on time.

➜ Send out the minutes from the meeting promptly and ask for feedback on the meeting.

Time-keeping

It's essential to be on time for meetings or appointments. Not only does it mean that you make the best use of your time, it shows that you appreciate that others have given up time to be there.

Here are some time-keeping tips:

➜ Check where you're going in advance and take a map and contact details with you.

➜ Plan your journey in advance and allow plenty of time – not only will you save money, but also last minute stress!

➜ Plan an alternative route in case there is a delay.

➜ If you're going to be late, let the person you're meeting know – phone them as soon as you get the chance, and let them know when you're likely to arrive. Give them the option of seeing you when you arrive or re-scheduling the appointment for another time.

Personal presentation

Most people judge your reliability and professionalism within the first 10 seconds of meeting you. Big decisions can be made simply on appearances.

Here are some ideas for putting your best foot forward:

→ Dress appropriately – judge the situation and the audience. For example, if you're taking a demo to a recording studio, then a business suit may not create the right impression.

→ Look smart and well-groomed – keep make-up and jewellery to a bare minimum. The same applies for nail polish – if it's chipped or badly applied, take it off.

→ Have everything that you need for the meeting to hand – preferably in a neat folder – so that you don't have to go rummaging through a bag at the meeting table.

→ Avoid wearing strong perfume or aftershave, which can be overpowering.

→ If you smoke, try not to have a cigarette before your meeting.

→ The way you hold yourself is important – if you stand up straight, you will appear more confident and people will respond better to you.

→ Look interested – when you're listening to someone, nod your head every so often to show you are interested. When speaking, refer back to relevant comments that have been made by others.

→ Don't be afraid to ask questions if you don't understand something.

Follow up

Set aside time every day to respond to actions from meetings you've been to during the day – you may only need 15 minutes after each meeting but the time you spend will show that you keep your promises and that you are a reliable person with whom to do business. The same applies to sending out minutes promptly after a meeting and following up on any deadlines that were agreed at the meeting. If you can respond before the deadline, so much the better.

'Most people judge you within the first ten seconds of meeting you'

My story

Lee Andrews, Impwood

I make and design furniture but, as a business, I am doing things I have never done before. It's been very handy having my mentor. It's a gift if someone is prepared to give you some time, so take what they say and use it.

When you are going to meet someone, you should change into smarter clothes and look more presentable. And you should do a bit of swotting beforehand. I have been to meetings and thought things could have gone so much better if I had been more prepared. When I was a kid, I used to lie a bit, but you just end up digging a bigger hole for yourself and looking stupid. You don't have to blag it if you do your homework, and just be yourself. It's also for your own sake. You don't want to turn up and find out that you are talking to the wrong person. It's a waste of time.

There are a lots of things you can do to get rid of stress and anxiety, like maybe going for a walk or doing an activity for 10 minutes to calm your nerves. It's good to step out of your environment every day. If I step away from something I am designing and do something different, it often means I actually save time, as I realise there is a simpler way of doing it.

I am also a retained fireman, which is useful. It's nice to have something else to think about. It enables me to be more sociable and communicative with people as I am not in the workshop all the time.

My mindset is different at work. At work I am decisive, but not so much at home. To be a creative force, you need to be able to take risks and be decisive. Most well known designers tend to be people that can take decisions and have faith in the consequences.

How and why to network

Building up a network of useful contacts is a must for new businesses. Remember that networking is a two-way process. If you spend enough time at events listening, being generous with offering information and help, and following up contacts, your efforts will pay off. You may find that at the beginning, you are putting in more than you get out, but it's worth keeping going.

It can be intimidating walking into a room full of strangers, and hard to know how to strike up a conversation. Questions like 'What brings you to this event?' or 'What sort of business are you in?' will help break the ice. Once you are in a conversation, it may feel awkward to end it, but if you are to make the most of the event, you will need to talk to more than one person. Don't be embarrassed – as it is a networking event, the other person may well be thinking the same thing! Good exit lines to use are: Do you know X? I'd like to introduce you, if you'll excuse me…

It's been great to meet you. Please excuse me, there's someone I need to meet over there.

Here are some other things to bear in mind:

→ Research the businesses and people expected to attend and have an idea of who you would like to meet.

→ If you're on your own, find someone else who is not talking to anyone and introduce yourself. If everyone is in groups, look for a group of people you would like to join and ask the event organiser to introduce you.

→ Don't interrupt if people are deep in conversation – listen to what is being discussed and wait for a break in the conversation to introduce yourself.

→ Stand near the buffet or drinks – but figure out what food it would be best to eat if you are going to be shaking a lot of hands or talking a lot.

→ Wear your name badge on the right lapel so that it's easy to see when you're introducing yourself.

→ Try to find some common business ground – ask people what they do and why they are at the event.

→ Have plenty of business cards with you.

→ Don't forget to ask for their contact details too – people can easily lose your card and promotional materials.

→ After the event, write notes on the back of the business cards to remember the conversations you've had.

→ Follow up with the contacts you think could be valuable in the future. You could send a friendly but professional e-mail attaching an article which you think they might find interesting.

→ Keep a contacts database – or an indexed file of business cards – so that you can easily look back on the contacts you've made, where you met them and what you talked about.

→ Be generous – put your contacts in touch with each other and share information that you think will be useful. It gives you an opportunity to get in touch again and build a relationship with a contact. You will also get a reputation for being helpful – you will never be alone at a networking event for long!

→ Finally, you won't always meet your best contacts at organised networking events. You may meet someone at a gym or when you're out shopping. Always make sure you look presentable, or slip into the conversation something about where you have been previously, to explain how you are dressed.

Time management

Managing your time is tricky when you're running a business and the only way to make sure you get things done is to learn how to prioritise tasks.

Here are some tips to help you get the most out of your time:

→ Keep track of meetings and to-do lists in a standard day-to-a-page diary. Make a list of the things you need to do each day, in order of importance, do the tasks in order and cross each one off as you complete it.

→ Know when you work best – some people work better in the morning and others in the afternoon – and tackle challenging projects when you're feeling most alert.

→ If you have several tasks to do that are equally important, tackle the thing you're least looking forward to doing – the other tasks will seem like a treat in comparison!

→ Limit distractions – if e-mails arriving in your inbox distract you, make a point of checking e-mails only once in the morning and once again in the evening.

'The only way to get things done is to learn how to prioritise tasks'

Know when to say 'no' – if you take on too much, you will disappoint people when you fail to meet the deadline.

 Know which tasks need more effort and which tasks you can spend less time on – and don't waste time on tasks that bring little reward.

 Under-promise and over-deliver – it's far better to overestimate how long a task will take and find that you complete the task earlier than promised than to give people unrealistic expectations.

Working from home

It can be tricky to work from home and to put yourself into work mode, with distractions like family, the TV, even the washing up, constantly there. Likewise, it's hard to switch off at the end of the day, and to draw the line under where the work day ends and home life begins. The key is in being disciplined:

 Start the day as you would a typical working day – set a routine, time for breaks and lunch and a time when you will stop working, and stick to it. Don't be tempted to check your e-mails one last time before heading to bed.

 Try to work in a quiet space where you're unlikely to be distracted – and even better, a space that you can close off when your working day is done.

Let personal calls go to voice-mail and respond to them when you finish working.

Talk the talk

Open questions

A question that cannot be responded to with simply 'yes' or 'no' – for example, 'How did you travel to the meeting today?

Closed questions

A question that can be responded to with simply "yes" or 'no' – for example, 'Have you two met before?'

Minutes

A written record of what decisions were made at a meeting that is then sent to the people who attended the meeting.

'The only thing that sets you apart from established companies is experience'

eight

Mentors and role models

Self-employment can be lonely. Unlike in the workplace, you're not a member of a team and you're not able to turn to someone more senior for support and guidance. Because the responsibility sits squarely on your shoulders, it's a huge challenge. Having a role model or a mentor can help take some of that weight.

Who is your role model?

Most of us could think of people who have inspired and motivated us – perhaps a well-known entrepreneur or a family member. Most successful entrepreneurs, when asked what inspired them to start their own businesses, will talk about someone who influenced them, whether through their enthusiasm, capacity to work, or success. You may already have a role model who you would like to be like. It might be that you admire a teacher who has played a big part in your life and you would like to be as patient, creative or as good a leader as they were. Or it might be that you would like to follow in the footsteps of Richard Branson because you admire his creativity and willingness to take risks.

'Think of people who have inspired and motivated you'

A role model is often someone who is not directly involved in your business, but someone who you can look to for an example of how you might want to run your business. Identifying someone who you think is successful and has achieved what you would like to achieve can help to give you direction and motivate you, both when times are good and not so good. A role model can have a big influence over you and your business. They can:

→ **help you define your business values** – for example, have you selected your role model because you have values in common? How have they built their values into their business and can you follow their example?

→ **help you to make difficult decisions** – you could put yourself in your role model's shoes and ask, 'What would Richard Branson do?' or 'How did Innocent take on its competitors?'

→ **help you to overcome challenges** – no role model has got where they are today without having faced some challenges, criticism and taken some risks – some of which have paid off, some of which have fallen flat. Become familiar with the mistakes your role model has made and what they learned from those mistakes. Not only will it help to prepare you for any challenges you might face, it will keep you positive when things are tough.

→ **help you choose a direction for your business** – for example, how has your role model spotted opportunities to take their business in a particular direction, how has it helped develop their business and what can you learn from the decisions they made?

Our story

Ben and Michael Dyer, The Altogether Company

We set up the Altogether Company in 2008. We take care of the enterprise requirements for schools, set out in the national curriculum. We do challenge days that inspire the students to consider self-employment, and gain transferable skills required for work, like communication and presentation skills.

Our funding came from The Prince's Trust, and our mentor there was Robin Evans. He has been fantastic and goes above and beyond. If we don't give him the finance figures, he chases us, which is good because we can be a bit scatty. We know the bottom line, but he really tries to keep us on top of it. He always calls me back if I leave a message, and makes time for us (that works both ways). He is our first port of call. We went to Colchester last year, and had a good day but had a couple of complaints about trivial things. We weren't used to that, so I rang him for advice as to how to improve things.

I look up to James Caan. I read his book – he started off in recruitment like me and his principles are similar to mine. He wanted to provide a fun and fast-paced working environment, as do we. He always buys into a person, even if the idea seems quite wacky, and that's what we say to the students on our days.

We're hoping to be the market leader in enterprise days within two years. So far, we have delivered to 10,000 students nationwide, but every secondary school in the country must provide enterprise days, so we have only scratched the surface.

What is mentoring?

Mentors are many things to different people – a positive role model, an adviser, an experienced friend, trusted family member – you may already have a mentor you turn to for support and advice.

Having a mentor to turn to can be very helpful and often free; many business support organisations offer free mentoring, whether in person or online, and some companies allow their staff time to volunteer as mentors in their communities. Here are some of the reasons why you might consider getting a mentor:

Two heads are better than one

Starting a business is a challenge for anyone, and nobody would expect you to know it all. A mentor can be particularly useful to you in starting and developing plans for your business because they can bring a whole host of skills and experience to the relationship that you can benefit from. If you know that you are not particularly strong on marketing, a mentor who understands this area could share their experience and knowledge with you, and advise you on the best action to take. Similarly, a mentor can help you to develop your entrepreneurial skills, rather than your knowledge of a particular sector – for example, money management.

A second opinion

It can be difficult to distance yourself from your business, but sometimes being involved in every detail, from start to finish, can mean that you miss things that are obvious to other people. A mentor can offer an impartial opinion and an outside perspective on your business. A mentor who may not have knowledge or experience of your particular sector might help you tackle a problem from a different angle – suggesting, for example, 'I know you've always done it like this, but why not try this?'

Been there, done that

You can't beat advice that comes straight from the horse's mouth. A mentor who can share what they have learnt from their own successes and mistakes can be a huge help, and save you a lot of money and effort, particularly in stopping you taking the wrong path. By having a mentor share their experiences – good and bad – it will help you to learn from any mistakes you make quicker and more easily, and learn to look at mistakes in a positive way.

A sounding board

Having an impartial person to talk to can be of huge value to your business. Think of the times when an idea you had instantly came to life after talking it through with someone. Or when a problem felt halved after talking to someone about possible solutions. Never underestimate the value of having a sounding board. It can be all too easy to think of your business as yours alone, but there are lots of things that can go into making or breaking a business: customers, suppliers, partners, and competitors. The more comfortable you are about asking for help and advice from people not directly involved in your business, the more capable you will feel to tackle the unknown.

A support

It can be difficult, particularly if you're running a business from home, to separate your work from your home life. Don't forget that you're an employee too, and you need to look after yourself the same way you would your business or staff. You are no good to your business if you work all the hours available and fall ill, or if you take no time out for self-development and training. A mentor can not only be someone who provides emotional support but someone who can give you an honest opinion about the personal and professional steps you may need to take to develop your business.

A network

A mentor with experience of running their own business is likely to have professional contacts that may be helpful to you. If a mentor has a professional relationship with a contact and can make an introduction on your behalf, it's a good head start. A mentor with whom you have a trusted and professional relationship will be more likely to introduce you to their network than a person they met once at a networking event.

'Don't forget you need to look after yourself the same way you would your business'

My story

Nathan Dicks, Learnthrumusic

There is a lot of support out there if you know where to look. As well as The Prince's Trust, I had help from the Welsh Assembly and funding from UnLtd, a charity that supports social entrepreneurs.

I have friends locally, one in particular who runs his own business. I can bounce ideas off him. I also have an adviser who helped us with the start-up process. I still see him roughly every fortnight, as I value his opinion. For me it is vital. I am confident, but I still like to hear from people with more experience than me. If I am running away with an idea, he can keep me in check, or approve of what I am doing. It's so easy to get carried away.

My company does what it says – it uses music to help students learn. I am competing in a multi-million pound industry, with companies like Letts Educational. It would be great to have someone with their experience on board.

I have been made a Dynamo role model, which is a scheme run by the Welsh Assembly. Young people like me who run their own businesses go into schools and talk to students about our business experiences, to inspire and encourage them to start their own business. I love it. At first, some of them don't want to know, but once you start talking to them, they start coming out of their shell. One time, I had six students who had to create a mock business and then present it. They were so nervous. I told them about how nervous I had felt when I had to receive my UnLtd award in front of 500 people, and how I had overcome it by thinking how lucky I was when there were people worse off than me. My students went on to win the event, and it was great for me, seeing them grow in themselves.

Finding a perfect match

It can be tempting to look for a mentor who has similar qualities and skills to you, but it often causes more problems to put, for example, two creative people in a room together. It's often a better idea to take a look at your own character, skills and experience and be honest about where you think you could do with help. If you know, for example, that you're great at coming up with ideas but not so great at seeing them through until the end, it's a good idea to find a mentor who will motivate you to plan and see something through.

Here are some more tips to help you find a suitable mentor:

→ Know whether you would like help to develop a particular skill – like time-keeping – or guidance on a specific sector or area of your business.

→ Be honest about what advice and guidance you need, and be prepared to share information about your business. When asking a person to be your mentor, be specific about the help you need.

→ Be realistic about the amount of time you can commit to being mentored, and decide whether face-to-face or online mentoring would suit you best.

→ Network. Ask your professional contacts if they know of someone who would make a good mentor and whether they would be willing to introduce you.

→ Select a mentor who is successful and has significantly more experience in the area you're looking to develop. It's easier to take advice from a mentor with a great deal of experience than from someone you would consider to be your equal.

What worked for me

Tony Elliott, Time Out

When I started out, I was working in the underground alternative press, so there were no role models in the established press that I respected. But there were people around who were doing stylish and innovative things, like *Oz* magazine, and they had an influence on me.

Although I wasn't fantastically close to my mother, she had a sense of what was and wasn't correct. She was a doctor and consultant to WHO and the Wellcome Trust, and was connected to important things that were going on in the world. I got a sense of right and wrong and who was doing good things and who was not from an early age, and it has stayed with me. From very early on, we refused to have anything to do with Robert Maxwell, even though he owned a huge number of printing firms in the UK at the time. If you do something devious, or manipulative, it will inevitably come back and bite you later down the line. You should behave towards people as you would like them to behave to you.

When it comes to advice, I have found that most accountants and lawyers will not take a risk or come up with anything original. In some ways, their advice is correct, because it is along the lines of 'cut costs', or 'make money'. But you kind of know all that, and need someone who can get inside your own head and see it from your perspective. That is a really important role of a mentor if you can find the right one.

For me to mentor someone, I have to be interested in what they are doing or I won't have enough enthusiasm. And I have to like them. It is also really important that they have the ability to listen. It's pointless if they ask for your advice and then wilfully ignore it.

The person you are mentoring needs to ask the right questions, so you can be clear about what is on their mind and what they are trying to achieve. It is always more helpful if they have a particular question to ask, rather than something wishy-washy. Sometimes if they are young and dealing with someone older and more experienced, they may be slightly in awe and embarrassed to ask what they think is a boring and obvious question. But actually the boring and obvious question is a good starting point.

How will mentoring work?

It's important to be clear about what mentoring is and isn't right from the start. Talk through with your mentor what you hope to gain from the relationship and ask them what they would like to gain in return. It's a good idea for both the mentor and the person being mentored (the mentee) to write down what they expect the relationship to be like – for example, how often you will meet, when is a good time to contact each other and how you will work together. That way, you can avoid misunderstandings and feel happy knowing what each person is responsible for doing.

Mentoring IS	Mentoring ISN'T
➔ Supporting and guiding a person to make decisions and take action for themselves.	➔ Telling a person what to do.
	➔ Offering consultancy.
➔ Mostly about listening.	➔ An opportunity to share your life story – rather it's about sharing relevant experiences in response to a question or challenge a person might be facing.
➔ Exploring and suggesting options.	
➔ Offering advice and guidance.	
➔ Helping a person to set and achieve realistic goals.	➔ Forcing a mentee to take particular decisions.
➔ Using personal experience in a positive way.	➔ Ensuring that person doesn't make any mistakes.
	➔ Taking personal responsibility for the mentee.
➔ Presenting an open, accepting and non-judgemental attitude.	➔ A personal relationship – a mentor shouldn't be like a parent or friend.

Tips for a successful mentoring relationship

A trusted relationship with a mentor won't come handed on a plate. Like anything worth having, it requires effort and commitment from both the mentor and the person being mentored.

There is no magic to running a business. The only thing that sets you apart from established companies is experience. Finding someone who can share the benefit of their experiences with you will help you through some of the more challenging – and lonely – times.

DO

- Agree some ground rules.
- Be there when you say you're going to be there.
- Have a positive outlook.
- Prepare before your meeting - what do you want to get out of the meeting?
- Be honest about the challenges you're facing and work with your mentor to tackle the causes of these challenges.
- Thank your mentor for their time.

DON'T

- Expect your mentor to solve all your problems for you.
- Finish a meeting without knowing what your next step is - what are you responsible for, when will you get it done, and what do you hope to gain from doing it?

'Make sure your business will flourish'

nine

Growing your business

Managing growth is a challenge for any business. To do it successfully, you need to make sure you create the right environment that means your business will flourish without putting pressure on you, your staff, your resources or your finances. It's important to think about your long-term aims, but to be flexible about how you can achieve your goals.

Are you ready for growth?

If your business is going to grow, it should always do so by design, never by accident. Grow too fast, without a clear plan, and you are more likely to run into cash flow problems. A business can look like it's flourishing, taking on lots of new customers and expanding into different areas – but if it takes on too much before it has enough money coming in, it will run into serious trouble.

If and when you spot an opportunity to grow your business, your first instinct should be to reach for your business plan. You shouldn't have to dust it off; your business plan is a working document and should be read at least once a year.

It's a good idea to do another SWOT at this point. Remember that doing a SWOT analysis is about looking at the *strengths* and *weaknesses* of your business and the *opportunities* and *threats* that could affect your market – but it's only an effective planning tool for growing your business if you turn the detail into actions.

Expansion could mean that you move into new or bigger business premises, employ staff or diversify into different markets. Regardless of what growth looks like for your business, planning for growth means returning to the first phase of business planning again. If you're planning to move into new and bigger business premises, you will need to understand and calculate the effect the higher fixed costs, rent, for example, will have on your profit. If you're planning to take on staff, you will need to calculate the cost of their salaries and benefits as well as the cost of equipping your business, for example, with office furniture, equipment, IT and telephone networks. And if you're planning to diversify into a different market, you will have to be confident that there is a need for your new product or service, that you understand the target market and that diversifying will make you money.

'Grow by design, never by accident'

Exploring new avenues

Diversifying what your business can offer customers can mean different things. It can mean:

→ offering new or related products and services to your existing customers – for example, you may choose to stock gifts and greetings cards in your florist

→ exploring new markets for existing products or services – for example, you may decide to sell gifts online as well as at your business premises

→ offering new products or services to a new target market – you may perhaps decide to start a completely different business that will mean researching a new product or service and a new target market.

To work out if and when to diversify, you will need to weigh up the risks and the benefits by researching the market and perhaps testing out your new offering. You will also need to plan how you will manage the additional costs as well as satisfy demand.

Diversifying with similar products or services and selling these to your existing customers is less risky than developing a brand new product or service for a different market. Selling similar products and services means that your energy and focus is less likely to be steered away from your existing business. It can also be easier to secure orders for your new product or service up-front, particularly if you are targeting your existing customers. That way, if your new venture is not successful straight away, your existing business will be able to support you while you grow.

My story

Chris Hooper, Crazy Combat Ltd

I originally thought about a paintball business, but switched to laser guns when I saw it was less stressful to run – cheaper insurance and running costs. Our first site was a concession in Flamingo Lands Theme Park. I bought nine guns originally, and from the first day we were mobbed.

We then built two more sites, on land we rented in caravan parks, which also went really well. We run the three sites as three separate limited companies, as it is better for tax (VAT) reasons. I carried on with Flamingo, while my brother ran the other two. We got up to 95 guns, but the trouble is that the contracts are changed annually. A new director has come in and is gearing the park towards pensioners, so he doesn't want us there. I had four full-time staff and around four part-time, and had to lay one off. My brother is looking for other sites to grow the business and use the guns we have spare. We are looking at putting up inflatables in the park and using the guns there.

I was asked to set up another, different, business at Flamingo Lands, next door to our own. I thought about it a lot but decided I would need more staff and would be flicking between the two. I enjoy laser guns so much and I wasn't sure about doing something new and running both at the same time. It would be a risk. I would be competing against myself. The new business would charge more, which would take money away from people. And I would have to employ more staff, which is bit of a problem. I need to have staff that I can trust and it is really hard to get them, especially as we are a seasonal business. In the end I decided to put the idea on hold until an opportunity comes up for a complementary business on the same site.

Moving up, moving out

Your business may outgrow its premises (or your home), particularly if you are diversifying and need more space or if you are taking on staff. Here are some things that may get you thinking about whether or not the time is right for a move:

→ **Shortage of space** – you don't have the space to store or make your product or you have to pay out money for storage space, which is forcing you to increase the price of your product or make less profit.

→ **Location** – there's an opportunity for you to be closer to suppliers and transport links or closer to your target market.

→ **Cost** – the cost of rent or rates has increased and you may be able to find cheaper premises.

→ **Assets** – you may want to invest in buying your own business premises rather than carry on paying rent.

→ **Staff** – you need to hire staff to manage extra workload and need more space.

My story

Craig Smith, The Printed Bag Company

I set up our business in our living room with one computer. But I started getting bigger clients like Coca-Cola who were calling me at home and could hear my little girl in the background – it wasn't great. We also never switched off.

With the rent, rates, and expenses that come with an office, it was a big thing to think about, but once I moved in, I found I was making more money. I was spending more quality time, as there were no distractions.

I have someone to do my accounts and books. Before, I was doing it on a Sunday and didn't have a clue. Then I took on another person for sales. I was doing everything myself and I couldn't do any more, but it was still a big leap. Before I took Paul on I calculated how much he would need to generate to more than pay for himself. I did that calculation on a part-time basis, but he actually became full time within three weeks. If I had my time again, I definitely would have taken Paul on sooner. We are now looking to get an apprentice.

In our second year, the credit crunch hit, and our suppliers were advised by their under-writers to start cutting credit. We had £25–30k credit with some suppliers, and overnight we were told to pay it back before we were put on stop. It was quite a wake-up call. Now, we try and get everything **pro forma**. I think we have lost three clients since doing that. Not bad, given that we now get paid for everything up front and we don't have to pay for 30 days.

A lot of our success is down to the relationship we have with printers, which means we can turn around orders very quickly. We pass a lot of work to them and always pay on time and don't ask for the impossible. If you pay on time, they will favour you over people who don't. Without them we wouldn't have grown as quickly.

When we first started, our adviser asked us for the cash flow. I had never heard of one. He said we would turnover £27k in our first year. I thought 'never from my living room'. In our first year we did £125k, and we are now on track for about £500k this year.

Managing your business

You will be used to knowing every detail of your business; you started it from scratch, you've played every role from accountant to salesperson and you've built it into a successful business that is ready for growth. It's natural to want to keep control, but if you continue to do everything and don't learn to hand over tasks, the danger is that you will spread yourself thinly and your business will suffer.

You will need to change the way you are used to working. You can start by:

→ **Knowing what to delegate** – know when a job can be done better or quicker by a sub-contractor or another member of staff.

→ **Knowing how to delegate** – be clear about the task you're delegating and what you expect the result to be. The person who has responsibility for the job will be able to make their own decisions based on the results you expect from the task.

→ **Taking responsibility for the right tasks** – it's up to you to decide on the direction of the business and provide leadership and to take responsibility when things go wrong.

'Delegate – if you continue to do everything, your business will suffer'

Subcontracting

As your business grows, you may find that you have to subcontract work to others if you don't have the time or the staff to complete the extra work. It's a particularly good idea to subcontract out smaller jobs, or jobs in which you have little or no expertise, like managing your accounts or IT, while you can concentrate on developing new projects.

Top tip

Using subcontractors can be a more flexible arrangement than hiring more staff but, if they work on your premises, make sure your insurance covers them.

You should think of your **subcontractors** as an extension of your business. Put as much time and effort into finding trustworthy and reliable subcontractors as you would do employees, because customers will expect the same standards from them as they have come to expect from your business. To help you find the right subcontractors:

→ ask them to submit a trial piece of work related to what you need them to do – for example, if you need them to complete some design work, ask them to submit a small selection of mock-ups

→ check references and **testimonials** from businesses that have used them in the past

→ check that their qualifications and their memberships to any associations are genuine and in date

→ draw up a contract or agreement between you and the subcontractor setting out what work needs to be done, any deadlines that need to be met, and the payment you have agreed.

Employing staff

People can make or break a business. Creating the right relationships with customers, partners and suppliers is vital to success and as your business grows, it will be impossible to be everywhere at once. Any staff you employ will affect the productivity of your business and the impression customers have of your business. You will need to employ people you trust, that understand your business, and that will share the responsibility of making it a success.

Hiring staff for the first time can be a daunting task and it is a big commitment. It's important to consider the alternatives to recruitment, which might suit you better. Think about:

→ subcontracting the work

→ changing your ways of working so that work is divided up more efficiently

→ getting temporary help from friends, family or a volunteer

→ taking on contract or temporary staff

→ training or promoting an existing member of staff to take on the work.

'People can make or break a business'

If, after considering your options, you are confident that you need to employ staff, you could start by drawing up a description of what the job will involve, including:

→ job title – it's a good idea to decide on a job title after you have written the job description and decided upon the main responsibilities of the role

→ type of role – for example, full-time, part-time or temporary and hours of work

→ main responsibilities and activities

→ who the employee reports to

→ pay and benefits

→ location and whether any travel will be necessary.

Now that you have thought about the type of job you have available in your business, it's easier to write a description of the sort of person you want to do the job. This is known as a person specification, and will detail their skills and qualifications, previous experience, and the personal attributes you would like to see – for example, hard-working, well organised.

Recruiting staff can be expensive but there are options that you can take to keep costs down. You can find potential candidates through:

→ **word of mouth** – talk to your existing business network, friends, and any other contacts

→ **colleges and universities** – placing an advert in a college or university newsletter can be a good way of recruiting people to fill a temporary role in your business, for example over the summer period

→ **internet** – search websites where potential candidates post their CVs for employers

→ **newspapers or trade publication** – place a job advert in trade publications if you are looking to recruit a person with specialist skills or qualifications

→ **local job centre**

→ **recruitment agencies** – it's important to research which recruitment agencies would be most effective at promoting the role you have available, for example, ask to see the CVs of the candidates they have on their books and references from other clients.

Writing a job advert – get it right

Placing job adverts can be costly – particularly if your advert isn't effective at attracting enough of the right people and you're forced to advertise again.

DO	DON'T
→ Consider whether your advert would work best in a local or national newspaper.	→ Make your advert difficult to read – avoid fancy graphics and fonts.
→ Compare and negotiate a good price for advertising space.	→ Use capital/upper-case letters.
→ Brand your advert.	→ Use clever or abstract headings – stick to the basics and always make it clear what you're advertising.
→ Make it clear what the job involves – if the job title doesn't make it clear, include a sentence briefly describing the role.	→ Give too much technical information about the job or the company – save that for the information and recruitment pack.
→ Use bullet points and bite-size paragraphs.	
→ Give a brief description of your company vision – for example, your key messages and the direction the business is heading in.	→ Use too many words to get your message across.
→ Involve the reader – refer to the reader as 'you', for example 'You will be an experienced and motivated manager…'	→ Focus your writing too much on the job and not enough on the person you're looking for.
→ Include the location of the job – and mention whether any travel is necessary.	→ Waste money on huge half-page or full-page spreads.
→ Make the deadline for responses clear and indicate how candidates can apply – for example, online or by post.	
→ Double-check your advert for spelling mistakes and formatting errors – any mistakes in your advert will not give a good impression to potential candidates.	

Interviewing — get it right

Interviewing is often just as nerve-wracking for the interviewer as it is for the candidate. Here are some tips to help you prepare for finding the perfect person for the job.

→ Keep a list of your reasons for interviewing or not interviewing candidates because you may be asked for feedback later. Don't choose not to interview someone because they have mentioned a disability on their application form.

→ Book a private room so that you won't be disturbed.

→ Decide whether you'll be interviewing the candidates one-to-one or whether you will have colleagues helping out.

→ Introduce yourself and anyone else you have helping you to interview.

→ Tell candidates that you will be taking notes during the interview.

→ Ask the same questions to every candidate so that you can make fair comparisons.

→ Give the candidate the chance to ask questions at the end of the interview.

→ Tell the candidate what they can expect to happen next – for example, when can they expect to hear, will there be a second round of interviews?

→ Ask the successful and unsuccessful candidates for feedback on the recruitment process – and be prepared to give feedback in return.

→ Store all personal information noted from the interviews in a secure place.

→ Don't just interview people who are like you – it's important that you recruit people with different experience and skills.

→ Don't choose not to employ someone on the grounds of race or religion, sex or sexual orientation.

What worked for me

Mike Clare, Dreams

Unless you are going to be a heart surgeon relying on your own skills, at some point you will need to take on staff as your company grows. And you'll certainly need to rely on them, so choosing the right employees is fundamental.

Finding someone you can get on with and work with is more important than academic qualifications. I ask myself have they got a CAP on their head – have they got Common-sense, Attitude and Personality? Some people are always miserable and moaning about the government, their neighbours, the police or whatever. Others are positive. It doesn't matter what the job is or at what level. If they are positive, chatty, smiley people, it counts for so much.

At an interview, you have to cut through normal interview questions to find out what really makes that person tick. You can ask things like: what would you do if you won £40k on the lottery; who do you admire; what was the last book you read; what was the happiest and saddest time in your life? You are trying to find out what they are really like, not the persona they try to present at the interview.

You can, hopefully rarely, be unlucky and get a round peg in a square hole. If it happens, it is better to address it early on – without being ruthless and bearing employment law in mind. It is better for the business and usually better for the individual as well.

Once you have taken people on, it's good to find out what motivates them and make a note of it, whether it's flexible working or wanting a window seat. Some staff like to suggest improvements to products or services, and for me that's great, as they hear from customers so much more than management do. Our delivery men changing into slippers at a customer's door when they deliver beds was a driver's idea. Before that, if they took their shoes off and walked around in socks, there were health and safety and smelly feet issues. It's a small thing, but customers regularly comment on it.

When it comes to money, if you pay 10–20 per cent above the average, you will normally get someone twice as good and have less staff turnover. We also try and make sure that everyone understands the company, our brand values and feels connected. We include a newsletter with all staff pay slips every month, so that their family can read it and know what is going on too. And we offer training where it is needed for the job. Listening to staff is important, so you can judge their mood. Happy Staff = Happy Customers = Successful Company.

Where to find more funds

As your business grows you may need to find extra money to invest in your business – for example, to finance new equipment or to buy stock for the increased trade coming through your business.

There are a number of potential sources of funding available.

Business Angels

Business Angels are wealthy individuals who invest their own money in businesses that are ready for growth in return for a share of the business. They will normally invest between £10k to £750k, and will often want to be involved in the running of the business. There are a number of networks where you can contact Business Angels to pitch for their investment. You should have developed your business plan to show that you have researched and tested your future plans and prepared an **exit strategy** or a plan for how you will respond if your plans don't work as well as you hope. It's a good idea to contact your local Business Angels network where you can arrange to have a practice run of your pitch before you go to an investment presentation meeting.

Venture capital funds

This money normally comes from private sector companies and wealthy individuals and is pooled together by investment companies. Venture capitalists will invest large sums of money – normally around £2m (although in the regions this can be much smaller) – in return for a share in your business. As well as investment, they will also provide a huge amount of expertise to your business. The disadvantage is that getting the funding can be a long and complex process, and the funds are normally less flexible than funds from Business Angels. Arrange to meet the investment funder or ask a Business Angel to introduce you. Again, you should have developed your business plan to show that you have researched and tested your future plans and prepared an exit strategy.

Expansion loans

Expansion loans are a good source of funding for businesses that are expanding or would like to do so. These loans allow you to invest in better equipment or a larger workspace. A bank will need to understand your business performance and how an expansion loan will be repaid before they lend you any money. Banks will also need to understand the length of the life of the business, the proposed plan for expansion and proof that expansion is necessary.

Next stop, the world

Once you are comfortable that your business has established itself in the UK market, it may be time to consider opportunities abroad. But the world is a big place and, before you start, you need to decide which would be the most appropriate markets. That means researching potential regions and considering whether your products are suitable for each area. You also need to consider, very carefully, whether you have the necessary resources, both in terms of finance and manpower, to start exporting. Taking on a new market is a big commitment and you need to be sure that your business is ready.

The first step is to carry out detailed market research to assess the target market. Exporting abroad is no different to first setting up your business in the UK – you need to know your customers and competitors. Find out how large the target market is, who they are buying from at present, who your competitors would be, how they operate and any other details about the way the industry works in the region. On top of this, you will also need to look at things specific to your target region, such as import regulations, packaging requirements and exchange rates.

Once you have done your market research, you can draw up an export plan that will match the reasons why you want to expand overseas with your ability to do so, and detail how you will put your plan into action.

Here are some of the things you should be thinking about:

→ Do you have the necessary financial resources and people to expand overseas without stretching yourself too thinly at home? Do you have people on board with the necessary expertise?

→ Do you know enough about the requirements of your chosen market – for example, adapting your product to meet local regulations and standards, or export payments?

→ Have you considered any language or cultural barriers that you might come across?

→ What costs are involved in terms of travel, distribution, production and advertising – are there overseas events or trade fairs that you could take part in?

→ Will you export indirectly using third parties or will you do it yourself?

UK Trade & Investment provide a number of different services to companies looking to expand abroad, and will be able to advise you on the steps necessary, wherever your chosen market may be.

If the right building blocks are in place, taking your business to its next stage should be an exciting time. Make sure you are thoroughly prepared and you will be able to seize the opportunities with both hands.

Talk the talk

Subcontractor

A freelance worker who carries out work for you but isn't directly employed by your business.

Testimonial

A statement, usually written, in which a person or business confirms that they were happy with a particular product or service.

Exit strategy

A plan as to the way in which you will end your involvement with your business.

Pro forma invoice

An invoice sent before goods have been supplied, which allows the buyer to raise a purchase order.

'Your business plan should prove to you that your business can succeed'

ten

Writing the business plan

A business plan will help you turn your idea into a reality. It gives an outline of your business, the market in which it will operate and how it aims to make money. It's a vitally important exercise that will hopefully show that your business has the potential to succeed.

Many people will write a business plan if they are looking for investment from a bank or business angel. But the most important reason is to prove to yourself that your business can succeed, and that you are not about to waste time, money and a lot of emotional heartache on an idea that will never get off the ground. Your plan should allow you to answer this question: why will your business succeed when so many others fail? Turning your idea into a reality, and being clear about how this will be achieved before you open your doors for business helps cut down on that risk. Your business plan can show you where your idea needs tweaking, once you have looked carefully at things like costs and competition, to help you on the right path.

As Andrew Dixon, founder of ARC InterCapital explains, there are three fundamental questions to a business plan – what, who, and how.

What is your product or service?

Who are you trying to sell to and in which market?

How will you reach them?

'Why will your business succeed when so many others fail?'

How long should it last?

'Your first plan may well not lead you to the endgame. The moment you deal with customers you learn something, and almost always have to adapt your plan,' says Dixon. There are many things that could make you change your assumptions of the business and the things you have written. It could be talking to customers, feedback from staff, what your competitors are doing, even luck. You shouldn't consider your business plan as a document set in stone that must never be changed and that you must follow to the letter. Its purpose is to guide and inform, so be prepared – and don't be afraid – to change it if needs be. The question to keep asking yourself is, does what I am doing make sense?

That said, it is good to keep an eye fixed on the future, and the further ahead you can see, the better. Try and review your plan every year, if not sooner. The reality is that it should be in the back of your mind all the time, and you will be constantly reviewing it in your head.

How simple should it be?

'You want your grandmother to be able to understand it, in no more than 10–20 pages,' is Dixon's view. People tend to overcomplicate business and there is no need. If you are unable to answer the 'what, who, and how' of your business in under a minute, then it may be that you are not doing the right thing. 'I have invested in 15–16 businesses,' says Dixon. 'The ones that are struggling most are the ones where I would struggle to explain exactly what they do. The most successful, I can tell you in 30 seconds what they do and how they do it, and most importantly why they are successful,' he concludes.

My story

Matthew Auckland, The Laughing Buddha

I knew I wanted to run an IT company, but until I did my business plan I didn't realise what my competitors did. By analysing their businesses, I saw they were already covering my sector, which was primarily business and building systems. I did my research and realised that home users were a better target. A lot of the bigger IT companies were either charging too much or not covering this market at all. I refocused the business and set myself up as a jargon-free service, giving friendly, honest advice.

The plan also made me focus on what I needed my investment for. When you decide to set up a business, you have grand ideas of a big office and expensive kit, but it's not necessary. I have a space at home that does the job nicely.

It took me about three–four weeks including research to put my 12 page plan together. I looked at it again pretty soon after I had secured my funding to tick off all the things I needed to achieve.

I readdressed it two years later, in order to look at short and long term targets. I wanted to see where I was, in order to determine whether I should be looking at other markets. Plans do evolve. You can change goals and go off in new directions as new avenues and markets open up. I have now entered the business market, for example, and realise that you can charge higher rates, but you can be waiting up to 60 days to get paid. Joe public will write you a cheque or pay cash, which is much better for a start-up.

I address the plan as events change, and as I feel the need. But at the beginning of every year, I take a few days out to look at it and any notes I have made, to prepare myself for the year ahead.

Your business plan should include the following sections:

→ **business description** – describing the products or services your business will provide and where the business will operate

→ **market and industry description** – with details of your market, customers and competitors

→ **personal details** – including relevant experience and training

→ **marketing plan** – setting out how you will promote your business and stand out from the competition

→ **pricing and sales analysis** – deciding your pricing policy and setting sales targets

→ **finances** – including the equipment you'll need to buy, the personal income you'll need to draw from the business, and forecasts of your cash flow for the first year.

Following the 'what', 'who' and 'how' rule, on the following pages is a checklist of things that you should think about and questions that you should be able to answer in each section of your plan.

'You shouldn't consider your business plan as a document set in stone'

Business description —WHAT are you selling?

➜ What are you actually selling?

➜ What is your Unique Selling Proposition – what will make your customers use your product or service rather than your competitors'?

➜ How can you build competitive advantage that will last – you may have a great idea but do you have knowledge, processes, or skills that others can't copy that will keep you ahead?

➜ How much will you charge – how have you come to this figure and how does this compare with your costs and profits?

Market and industry description —WHO are you trying to sell to?

➜ Will there be enough customers to buy your product, and will there be further growth down the track? There is no point moving into a declining industry, such as vinyl records, unless you can find a specific niche within it.

➜ Who are the customers, and what problem are you solving for them?

➜ Who is making the buying decisions – is it really the customer or perhaps a decision-maker on behalf of the customer?

➜ Is there repeat business?

➜ Who will be your first genuine customer beyond friends and family?

➜ How will you acquire them and how much will that cost?

→ Are they prepared to pay the price you have set and in the volumes you thought they would?

→ When will they pay? Depending on the type of business, you may not be paid for 30 or 60 days.

→ How much do you have to spend to make sure you get repeat business and not just a one-off sale?

→ How powerful are your competitors and how many are there?

→ What do they offer – what is their USP?

→ What have they done well in the past?

→ Could there be an entry from a new industry player?

→ How many buyers are there in the industry – if there are many, there are lots of opportunities. But if (as an extreme example) you make military aircraft, it will be hard to break in.

→ How many suppliers are there – if there are many, you will have more ability to negotiate.

→ When will you have to pay suppliers? As a new business, you will not have a credit rating with suppliers and may have to pay in advance, even though your customers are not paying you for 30–60 days.

→ Is it a competitive industry with everyone working on small margins or is there room for new market entrants?

Personal details – HOW will you reach them?

Now you've identified who you're selling to, you need to think about how you reach them.

➜ How will you promote your business – through advertising, direct sales, networking?

➜ Put yourself in the shoes of your potential customer or client – what will have the greatest impact?

➜ What contacts do you have in the industry – do you know your competitors, your customers, good staff to hire, good suppliers to buy from?

➜ Where will you sell from – home, rented premises, by mail order or the internet?

➜ How much will you spend on promotion and when? Timing can be key. For example, if you are promoting door to door, think about the time when people are most likely to be at home.

Remember that you represent your product or service:

➜ What are your skills? Focus on your strengths rather than trying to overcome your weaknesses.

➜ What qualifications, training and interests do you have and how can you use these to best effect to reach your target market?

Sorting your finances

The last stage of your business plan is to figure out how much money you'll need to start your business and keep it running each month. Start with your costs, which will be the equipment, staff and services you need to run your business. These might include:

→ equipment

→ materials

→ stock

→ employee costs

→ rent, rates and utility bills

→ business repairs and maintenance

→ marketing costs

→ legal and professional fees

→ IT equipment

→ loan repayments and interest

→ postage and stationery

→ insurance

→ telephone bills

→ vehicle and travel expenses.

Put this information into your cash flow forecast, as described in Four. To remind you, this is your expectation of the flow of money coming in to (cash in) and going out of (cash out) your business every month, and will help you work out how much cash will be available in the business month by month.

Then consider your living expenses and calculate how much money you need to take out of the business to live on. Work this out by detailing your monthly minimum personal expenditure – including things like rent, phone and utility bills and family expenses – and any income or state benefits you are receiving.

My story

Nicola Heldt, Dance professional

I work as a specialist dance coach in schools, and also dance myself, choreograph shows and music videos, and manage a band – in fact everything to do with performing arts.

It was hard setting aside time to do a business plan as I am so used to moving about. But it was so important. It helps you work out: is it going to be worth it putting blood, sweat, and tears into getting this going, or is there no market, or too many competitors? And if there are loads of competitors, is there a way to be better than them?

I had to put together the costs of delivering education workshops on a spreadsheet. Working out the costings took time, as you need to do your research. You don't want to overcharge or undersell, but it's hard to put a price on yourself. Competitors varied between £300–£1000. I tried to make my prices flexible, by offering half days as well.

No one showed me how to use a spreadsheet, I had to teach myself. If I didn't know how to do something, I would try and find a website to show me. In the end, I put myself on a computer course. I didn't want to spend the money as it could have gone towards buying music or props. But it has really helped. You can save loads of time.

Now my mum wants to set up her own business as a mosaic artist and I am helping her. She's not business-minded and I can see the frustration in her, as she just wants to do it. I think we all feel like that, just wanting to get on, but I tell her to spend a couple of hours on her business plan each week and it won't seem so bad. She knows she has to do it so that she can work out whether it is worth her going into business, or keeping it as a hobby.

Your business plan is the most important document that you will need. With your plan in your hand, not only can you prove to potential customers and investors that you have a viable business, you will have the confidence to move forward and take the next step, knowing that you have worked out how your idea can become a reality.

'Understand how your plans can become a reality'

'Just get out there and do it'

Conclusion

No one ever said that running a business would be easy. There will be challenges and times when you question what you are doing. You will have to work hard, and be incredibly passionate about what you do. There may be some setbacks or adjustments and it may even be that your original business idea is not the business that you end up running. But the payback will be huge. Creating and running your own business is immensely rewarding, and something you can be very proud of having achieved. Completing the journey from an idea in your head to your first paying customers will be incredibly exciting.

The most important thing to remember is that you don't have to do it alone. There are plenty of people who will be happy to help, whether they are business advisers, trade associations, mentors, people you respect – sometimes even competitors! Never be afraid or embarrassed to ask for help. The worst that can happen is that they say no. There are also lots of online resources and books that can help, as you can see from the Directory.

The hardest part of starting a business is actually getting started. If, after reading this book, you think you've got what it takes, just get out there and do it. Make it happen.

Directory

One: Starting a business

Business Link

www.businesslink.gov.uk

Official Government website that provides business support.

The site includes BSI Grants and support directory. This directory allows you to search for potential sources of help with starting up, running or developing your business. Type 'Grants and support directory' into the search tool.

There is also information on how and why to set up a social enterprise. Type 'Social Enterprise' into the search tool.

CIC Regulator

www.cicregulator.gov.uk

For information on community interest companies.

Small Business Journey

www.smallbusinessjourney.com

For information and advice on business values.

Chartered Institute of Marketing

www.cim.co.uk

For helpful market research reports, while the market research fact file also has some good places to go to for more detailed advice.

Market Research World

www.marketresearchworld.net

For resources to help you carry out research.

Small Business Advice Service

www.smallbusinessadvice.org.uk

For free and independent advice and guidance for entrepreneurs starting or running a small business.

Further reading

Barrow, Colin, *Starting a Business for Dummies* (Wiley, 2007).

The Financial Times Guide to Business Start-Up.

Ashton, Robert, *How to Start Your Own Business for Entrepreneurs* (Prentice Hall, 2009).

Ashton, Robert, *How to be a Social Entrepreneur* (Capstone/Wiley, 2010).

Germain & Reed, *A Book about Innocent: Our Story and Some Things We've Learned* (Penguin, 2010).

Two: Forming a business

British Business Angels Association

www.bbaa.org.uk

For help with funding.

Design Council

www.designcouncil.org.uk

For general advice on branding, go to the resources and events section, and click on the business section.

Business Link

www.businesslink.gov.uk

For information on naming a Limited Company or a Limited Liability Partnership, type LLP into the search tool.

Companies House

www.companieshouse.gov.uk

All limited companies trading in the UK must be registered at Companies House.

J4B Grant

www.j4bgrants.co.uk

Comprehensive information on government grants for both business and voluntary groups and a database of organisations that provide business advice.

Shell LiveWIRE

www.shell-livewire.org

Shell Livewire offers a fully interactive website with a huge range of information on starting a business including a social network and discussion forum.

Prime

www.primeinitiative.co.uk

Promoting and supporting self employment and enterprise for people aged 50+.

NESTA

www.nesta.org.uk

Business start up support for creative businesses.

everywoman

www.everywoman.com

everywoman is the UK's leading provider of training, resources and support services for women in business. They work to increase the number and raise the status of women in the UK economy, using their experience and expertise to help women achieve their aspirations and realise their business and career ambitions.

Three: Marketing and sales

Upmystreet

www.upmystreet.com

For sourcing facts and figures about local areas including local businesses and facilities.

Office for National Statistics

www.statistics.gov.uk

Government agency that publishes statistics relevant to the UK ranging from employment and education to travel and tourism figures.

Survey Monkey

www.surveymonkey.com

A free online resource for designing, sending and evaluating surveys.

Newspaper Society: The Voice of Local Media

www.newspapersoc.org.uk

Find out about local newspapers, their circulation and how to feature in their pages.

Joint Industry Committee for Regional Press Research

www.jicreg.co.uk

A good resource for researching circulation figures for regional press.

Advertising Standards Authority

www.asa.org.uk

The Advertising Standards Authority is the UK's independent regulator of advertising across all media including TV, internet, sales promotions and direct marketing.

Information Commissioner

www.ico.gov.uk

A good resource for checking the legal implication of direct marketing and central registers where people have registered their preferences for receiving direct marketing.

Direct Marketing Association

www.dma.org.uk

DMA provide free legal advice to businesses delivering direct marketing campaigns.

Committee of Advertising Practice

www.cap.org.uk/The-Codes.aspx

This lists all the codes (do's and don'ts) of advertising.

Further reading

Scott, David Meerman, *The New Rules of Marketing & PR* (Wiley, 2009).

Brooks & Mortimer, *Marketing for Dummies* (Wiley, 2009).

Middleton, Simon, *Build a Brand in 30 Days* (Wiley, 2010).

Denny, Richard, *Selling to Win* (Kogan Page, 2009).

Maslen, Andy, *Write to Sell: The Ultimate Guide to Great Copywriting* (Marshall Cavendish, 2009).

Four: Managing your money

HMRC Her Majesty's Revenue and Customs

0845 900 0444

For help and general advice from HMRC on self-assessment.

Financial Services Authority

www.moneymadeclear.fsa.gov.uk

Straight-forward factsheets covering everything you need to know about borrowing money and basic bank accounts.

Business Debtline

www.bdl.org.uk

For advice on how small businesses can deal with late payments.

Further reading

Yates, Jonathan, *Freesourcing: How to Start a Business with No Money* (Wiley, 2009).

Barrow, Colin, *Practical Financial Management* (Kogan Page, 2006).

Five: Where to work

Nominet

www.nic.uk

The UK regulator for all domain names ending in .co.uk

InterNIC

www.internic.net

The regulator for all other domain names.

Cynthia Says

www.cynthiasays.com

A software portal that will test your website for usability and accessibility – and it's completely free to download.

Royal Institute for the Blind

www.rnib.org.uk

RNIB has guidance on making materials, premises and website content accessible to the blind and visually impaired.

SiteImprove

www.siteimprove.co.uk

Regularly quality checks your website for accessibility issues, misspellings and broken links.

Google Analytics

www.google.com/analytics

A free online tool that allows you to analyse data for free.

Internet Advertising Bureau UK

www.iabuk.net

A website that provides you with information on different internet marketing methods, consumer research and case studies and key internet marketing providers.

Business Rates

www.mybusinessrates.gov.uk

For clear no-nonsense information on business rates.

Further reading

Packer, Nigel T., *Internet Marketing: How to Get a Website that Works for Your Business* (Right Way, 2008).

Six: The legal bit

Directgov

www.direct.gov.uk

You can find your local authority.

Business Link

www.businesslink.gov.uk

Click on 'your business sector.' Type in the sector that you are working in, and you will be given a list of the regulations, licences, standards and trade bodies relevant to your business.

Financial Services Authority

www.fsa.gov.uk

Tel 0845 606 1234

Click on the FSA register to find an authorised insurer.

Information Commissioner

www.informationcommissioner.gov.uk

www.ico.gov.uk

Tel 01625 545745

You can find more information about data protection, along with details of whether you need to register your business, and apply for an information pack.

Intellectual Property Office

www.ipo.gov.uk

Tel 0845 9 500 505

This gives explanations and advice on intellectual property.

The Department of Trade and Industry

www.dti.gov.uk

Tel 0870 150 2500

Offers guidance and practical factsheets on employment law.

ACAS

www.acas.org.uk

Tel 0845 747 4747

Another good source of information on employment issues.

The Trading Standards Institute

www.tradingstandards.gov.uk

For information on consumer protection.

Office of Fair Trading

www.oft.gov.uk

Food Standards Agency

www.food.gov.uk

Further reading

The Essential Business Guide (Essential Business, 2008).

Seven: Selling yourself

Further reading

Templar, Richard, *The Rules of Work* (Prentice Hall, 2009).

McGee, Paul, *Self-Confidence* (Wiley, 2010).

Fried, Jason, *ReWork: Change the Way You Work Forever* (Vermillion, 2010).

Arden, Paul, *It's Not How Good You Are, It's How Good You Want to Be* (Phaidon, 2003).

Eight: Mentors and role models

Horse's Mouth – Online Coaching and Mentoring Network

www.horsesmouth.co.uk

An online network of coaches and mentors providing advice to entrepreneurs.

Further reading

Rachel Bridge, *How I Made It* (Kogan Page, 2009).

Blanchard & Johnson, *The One Minute Manager* (HarperCollins, 2004).

Nine: Going for growth

The UK Trade & Investment

www.ukti.gov.uk

The UK Trade & Investment Accessing International Markets programme can provide support and help in planning your entry into new overseas markets, including market research.

British Business Angels Association

www.bbaa.org.uk/portal

Official trade website promoting angel investment funding for businesses in the UK.

British Venture Capital Association

www.bvca.co.uk

Official website for members, venture capitalists and trusts which can be accessed for information on funding for growth.

The start-up donut

www.startupdonut.co.uk

Free advice, tools and resources including a free monthly subscription e-newsletter.

Benchmark Index

www.benchmarkindex.com

An online tool to use to benchmark your business and plan for the future.

Further reading

Blyth, Alex, *How to Grow Your Business for Entrepreneurs* (Prentice Hall, 2010).

Ten: Writing a business plan

Bplans.co.uk

www.bplans.co.uk

Lots of business plan templates and advice from business planning experts.

The Prince's Trust

www.princes-trust.org.uk

Business plan template and financial spreadsheets available to download.

Acknowledgements

A huge number of entrepreneurs and people at The Prince's Trust and Wiley have made this book happen.

First of all we'd like to thank Nina Prosser at The Prince's Trust and Jo Russell, who were excited right from the start about the idea of making The Trust's years of experience and inspiration in helping people set up businesses available to a wider audience. Without Nina and Jo working flat out for several months on shaping the advice and gathering the entrepreneurs' stories, this book would not exist. The book also owes a huge amount to Hayley Pannick at The Prince's Trust who was a linchpin throughout the project and who showed huge enthusiasm for the project all the way through. We'd also like to thank Nicola Brentnall and Anthea Jackson at The Trust for their advice on the legal chapter. Thanks also to Charlotte Ridley, Laura Garbas and Sarah Bullerwell in the marketing team and Suzi Price in the publicity team, Charlotte Reichwald for securing fantastic support from many of The Trust's valued Enterprise Fellows, and Sophie Beesley for putting up with Nina while she was researching and writing and being a huge support, fountain of knowledge and trusted proof-reader.

At Wiley and Capstone we'd like to thank Ellen Hallsworth, who had the idea for the book; Megan Varilly and Julia Bezzant in the marketing team, Caroline Baines in publicity, Grace O'Byrne who brought the whole project together and Oliver Arnott whose legal expertise helped to get this book off the ground.

The forewords from HRH, the Prince of Wales, Charles Dunstone and Lisa Dunlop do a fantastic job of showing what the book is about and demonstrating the life-changing work that The Prince's Trust does.

223

What makes this book different as a business start-up guide are the amazing stories of the young people who've gone out there and done it with the help of The Prince's Trust. We owe a huge 'thank you' to Lee Andrews, Matthew Auckland, Nathan Dicks, Justin Douglas, Ben Dyer, Michael Dyer, Natasha Faith, Matthew Harris, Nicola Heldt, Chris Hooper, Nash Hunter, Jessie Jowers, Lorna Knapman, Lee Lamb, Mark Livsey, Lucy Mann, Carlo Montesanti, Michelle Myers (and her children, Madeleine Myers and Amelia Myers), David Scott, Craig Smith, Nigel Tait, Kate Trussell, Claire Van Looy, Semhal Zemikael.

The Prince's Trust's Enterprise Fellows also bring this book to life with their advice about what works. We'd like to thank James Caan, Mike Clare, Tony Elliott, Nick Jenkins, Claire Locke, Geoff Quinn, Tim Roupell, Sarah Tremellen and Ben White for sharing their stories, and to Andrew Dixon, for all his advice and guidance on how to put together a business plan.

Beauty Secrets
Tel: 02890 315445

Parcel Partners

www.parcelpartners.co.uk

Bee Guardian Foundation CIC

www.globalbeeproject.org

PC People UK

www.pcpeopleuk.com

La Diosa

LA DÍOSA
LONDON

www.ladiosa.co.uk

Nine Months

www.ninemonths.co.uk

Joseph Lamsin Jewellery

JOSEPH LAMSIN
JEWELLERY

www.josephlamsin.com

Eco-Kids
www.eco-kids.org.uk

Teme Valley Care Ltd

www.temevalleycare.ltd.uk

Love Food Festival

www.lovefoodfestival.com

fall off the WALL

Creative design & production for print and digital media

www.falloffthewall.com

N Tait Services
Tel: 01732 852288

Kensho Extended Schools Service

www.kenshokarate.net

Phoenix Roofing & Flooring Contractors Ltd

www.phoenixroofingcompany.
co.uk

Impwood
www.impwood.com

The Altogether Company

Enterprise days for Schools

www.enterprise-days.co.uk

Rewise Learning (trading as LearnThruMusic)

Fast-Track Your Learning.

www.learnthrumusic.co.uk

Crazy Combat

www.crazycombat.co.uk

The Printed Bag Shop

www.theprintedbagshop.co.uk

The Laughing Buddha

The Laughing Buddha
IT Solutions

www.youandtheweb.co.uk

Nicola Heldt
Tel: 07880 888802